CLASSROOM MAGIC

Amazing Technology for
Teachers and Home Schoolers

BY
LINDA LLOYD

Metamorphous Press
Portland, Oregon

Published by

Metamorphous Press
P.O. Box 10616
Portland, OR 97210-0616

Copyright © 1990 by Linda Lloyd
Editorial and Art Direction by Lori Stephens
Printed in the United States
ISBN 1-55552-014-6

Sixth Printing March 1994

To David

With thanks to my teacher, John Grinder, who inspired and encouraged me in the writing of this book. I stand on his shoulders to push his work forward. Thanks also to Richard Bandler and Leslie Cameron-Bandler, who, with John Grinder, have developed, used, and so eloquently taught principles of Neurolinguistic Programming^{TM}. I also thank Vrle Minto for his permission to include his techniques from Alpha Truth Awareness. And thanks to Gloria Striewski and Jackie Lichty for their interest, encouragement and practical help. I also thank Ellen Myers for her valuable suggestions and long hours of typing. And a special thanks to my son, David, who encouraged me and taught me as only a growing young person can.

CONTENTS

Contents of Activities

Introduction

After teaching for ten years, I realized I no longer looked forward to each day with my students. I had done all I knew to maintain effective discipline, create dynamic lessons, motivate my students, and become interested in my work. In my searching, I attended workshops, listened to tapes, and read books. I discovered that we do not know all there is to know in any area of life, especially with children and how they learn! I began using the new techniques and found that the children became more uniquely individuals to me, and teaching became a personal challenge to increase my skills. I'm now a learner with my students, learning as much from them as they do from me. And with this, my enthusiasm had returned.

I share with you now some of the techniques I've learned and used. My hope is for you to rediscover your own joy of learning as you use these daily lesson plans. Make this your theme for the coming year, as you rediscover new ways of communicating with, teaching to, and learning from your students.

How To Use This Plan Book

Teachers are doing a remarkable job in these changing times—and yet they are often thinking they should have done more. They want to help their students but don't always know how. Most kids want to behave and learn. They want a chance to be successful and to like themselves. Both students and teachers are doing the best they can with what they know. The ideas and exercises in this book are designed to help us expand knowledge and awareness to include more choices in thinking and behaving. All the ideas aren't for everyone. Use what fits you and your style of teaching, so you can do better what you already do well. Remember that a change implies a period of time while things will seem different. Be glad—this lets you know you are changing.

To begin, record some of your past successes as a teacher: lessons that went well, children you reached and helped, great bulletin boards, creative lessons . . .

List 10 successes here.

Yea!

1._____

2._____

3._____

4._____

5._____

6._____

7._____

8._____

9._____

10._____

As you use this book to stimulate more of your great ideas, keep these past successes in mind and continue to build upon them.

Continue to build success upon success until you have the classroom you've dreamed of. Take some time to write or draw your dream classroom here.

Include anything you think you can achieve.

Keep your dream in mind as you are planning and teaching. Act as though you already have it—creating it as you do.

The following are some ideas that will be included in this workbook.

You are busy teaching many things in an already crowded schedule; therefore most of the activities in this book are short and fun. They can be used as a change of pace activity, a 5 minute filler, a free time activity, a recess game, or in many other ways. Use this plan book as you use your daily plan book.

Write in it

underline and circle things

Use it as a springboard for your own creativity

make changes in it

add or delete ideas

Coordinate this book with your daily plan book, referring to the pages and activities you will be using from this resource book. Keep this book from year to year. . . make it your personal planning and activity book, reflecting your own philosophy of learning.

Write to me and tell me your dreams and experiences. I can learn from you, too!

Linda Lloyd
1322 East Lake
Novi, MI 48377

THIS SPACE IS FOR YOU!

WEEK 1

Memory Made Easy

Children "remember" by auditory, visual, or kinesthetic (feeling or emotional) reminders. So if they put information into their "memory banks" in all three modes, they will "connect" with the memory whether they are searching for it in the auditory, visual, or kinesthetic channel.

You have noticed children looking upward toward the ceiling as if searching for answers up there, or their eyes darting from side to side as if to see inside their ears, or the child who wiggles around when asked to remember something. They are searching visually, as in looking at the ceiling; auditorily, searching near their ears; and kinesthetically, by moving as if to reproduce the body position in which they learned the information, or how they felt when they learned it.

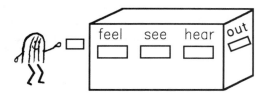

Children often choose one way of remembering and use that almost exclusively until you teach them to use all three ways. So if you teach only one way (by lecturing, for example), you will effectively reach only those students whose preferred way is auditory.

Use the chalkboard, use charts, graphs, and drawings to represent and coordinate with your lecture material. Get the children involved in role playing or involved emotionally in the material. When children are involved in all three modes—auditory, visual and kinesthetic—they will remember the information and ideas better no matter which mode they prefer using or if they are now using all three.

Teach the following lessons to convince yourself of this, or adapt some lessons you are already planning to teach to include all three methods of presentation. Notice what happens, and give yourself a pat on the back for trying something new.

Monday—Learning Names

Tell the children you will teach them a surefire way to remember names. Tell them to (1) shake hands, while they (2) imagine the person's name written on their forehead, and (3) say "Hi, (name)!" Then, whatever their memory cue is, it will bring back the person's name. Let the children practice with each other or with you. Give them time to comment on their success.

Tuesday—Auditory Memory—Songs

Remember some songs you used to sing when you were their age—songs you really enjoyed. Teach some to the kids. If there are actions to the songs, that's even better. Teach in all three channels: Auditory, Visual, Kinesthetic. Learn a new song a day until you have a classroom repertoire of songs. Sing them whenever your students need a change of pace or you have a few extra minutes. Let them teach you their favorite songs, too.

For example, if you are teaching the song, "The Itsy Bitsy Spider," have the words written on the chalkboard for them to look at as you sing the song and demonstrate the motions. You may teach the motions separately while humming the song, before putting it all together.

The itsy bitsy spider
went up the water spout
Down came the rain and
washed the spider out
Out came the sun and
dried up all the rain
and the itsy bitsy spider
went up the spout again.

Wednesday—Visual Memory— Camera Game

Tell the children their mind can be used as a camera. They can "take a picture" and then "see" the picture later in their mind.

Follow these steps:

1. Hold up a care with a **simple** design, combination of numbers and/or letters.

e.g. OXA YXTO 65321 5AB8R

2. Remove the picture. Pause. Say "Print it!" Tell them to look for the picture they put in their mind. Give them time to write it.

3. Hold the card up again and tell them to check it. Give them time to check it **and** to correct it to look like the picture. Tell them to correct it in their minds also.

It is necessary to teach students to transfer skills to the content areas in which they can use them. Many teachers believe that when they teach a skill or process, the students will automatically pick it up and begin using it in other areas. The students may be so concerned about learning the content that they aren't aware of having learned the skill, let alone think of ways to use it. Teach your students to transfer skills, or build a bridge, to other subject areas. Tell them they have learned a new skill and review the steps of the skill to make them more aware of it. Then discuss how they can use the skill when they study spelling words, learn math facts, or memorize maps. Give some examples and play the game using this new content. Ask them to think of other ways they can use this skill. Have them imagine themselves using this new skill in one content area, then another.

Imagine yourself teaching skill transfer, or bridging, whenever you teach a new skill, relating the skill to other content areas where they can successfully use it.

This exercise will strengthen skills needed in spelling and memorizing things such as math facts. NOTE: Children who say the name of what they are seeing will generally remember more.

VISUAL * * AUDITORY * * MOTOR * * EMOTION"

Affirm to yourself, "I will teach to the **whole** child!"

Thursday—Kinesthetic Memory—Motor Task

Give the students a motor task, such as writing their name backwards, with their non-dominant hand, or ask them to copy a complicated design. Have them do it once. Then have them copy or trace the original design five times. Tell them to notice the feelings in their arm and hand as they trace it. Then have them try it again. Notice the improvement. Their body has "remembered" the movements.

Kinesthetic also implies emotions—as well as motor awareness. When children are highly charged emotionally, they will learn with more impact. Experiment with fun and learning. Create exciting, involving lessons and notice your students' responses and learning rate.

Friday—Memory—Progress Through Time

Ask them to draw a picture and/or write a story. Ask them to remember ahead to when they can do it perfectly. Have them write or draw again. Ask them to compare the two and see what they are growing toward. Tell them to keep in their mind, while they are doing their work this year, the perfect paper they will achieve.

You can save these until the end of the year so they can compare and notice their progress. Have them also do work in other content areas to save and compare.

More learning takes place when a person is totally involved—emotionally, visually, auditorily, and kinesthetically. Relax and remember how much fun you used to have and the things you learned while having fun. Create that experience for the children you are teaching this year.

Affirmations

We create our reality with our thought. If we want to change something in the "real world," we do it first in our minds. We can change our conscious thoughts, but it's not so easy to change our unconscious thoughts. By repeating an affirmation—a positive phrase—we discover our unconscious reactions to the positive thought. Keep repeating the affirmation, just noticing the internal responses. When the responses begin to be in agreement the affirmation, our belief is changing and changes will begin to happen in the outer world as well. If you notice one persistent contradictory thought, create an affirmation designed to change it. For example, your original affirmation is, "I will teach to the whole child," and you persistently contradict it with the idea that "school should be hard work." Create and use an affirmation such as, "Children learn better when they are involved and enjoying it." When you have accepted this affirmation, then go back to the original one, "I will teach to the **whole** child."

Week of _____

As you read these ideas, think of variations or other ideas. Write them here, and in your plan book.

MONDAY	Learn names	Other things to memorize
	Time: _____	
TUESDAY	Song	Other songs
	Time: _____	
WEDNESDAY	Camera Game	If you forgot to make the cards, do it on the chalkboard and then cover it. Make it up as you go along.
	Time: _____	
THURSDAY	Motor Task	Other motor tasks to practice
	Time: _____	
FRIDAY	Papers to save	Other content areas to save papers or test in
	Time: _____	

WEEK 2

Create Your Own Self-Fulfilling Prophecy

Recognize the power of your beliefs as in the case of the self-fulfilling prophecy. In one study, a group of children who tested in the normal range on an I.Q. test were divided into two groups and given to two teachers. One teacher was told she had the "high" group and the second teacher was told she had the "slow learners." In a retest at the end of the year, the first group scored an average of 20 points higher.

What are your beliefs about your group? If it's true that they will only be able to achieve as high as you believe, how high can you raise your beliefs?

Monday—Beliefs

Think of your beliefs about your students. Begin to believe the best for them. Set your goals high and image each student as having achieved them. Imagine your students as they'll be at the end of the year—with all they've learned, how they've grown, with all their independence and skills. Take some time to do that now and again each day this week.

Tuesday—Troublemakers

Very early in the year, teachers tend to discover who will be the leaders, helpers, average students, and troublemakers in their class. ("Every year I have three troublemakers!" says Miss Grundy. And sure enough, she does!) Today, be aware of those students you've picked as troublemakers. Image their change into responsible, capable students. Then continue to see them that way. Watch them grow toward your image.

Each time one of your students behaves as if he's trying out for the position of troublemaker, REFUSE to see him that way. Refuse to label him. Remember that he wants to learn and be loved too. He's doing the best he knows how to get what he thinks he needs. Teach him another, more appropriate way.

When you're tempted to go into the faculty room to tell the other teachers what Johnny did this time, remember that you will get what you create, and ask yourself what you really want.

Wednesday—Believe—Children Want To Learn

Contrary to what you might sometimes think, children really do want to learn. Try and stop them! They are eager and learning all the time. They may be so turned off to school that they do their learning "outside"—but they're learning! This year, image your whole class as children who want to learn. (This could seem, at first, to be one of the most unbelievable things you've ever pretended—do it anyway.) Then notice your students' desire to learn. Use this desire. Teach students to be as excited about learning as they are about their outside activities. Build a bridge from their interests to your content area. You'll be as successful doing this as you believe you can.

Thursday—Believe—Children Have Everything They Need

Almost without exception, your students were born with everything they need to learn, grow and develop into capable, functioning human beings. These skills and resources may not be evident yet, or they may not be used at school, but they exist.

You've seen children like the one who can't remember to carry the tens when he adds, yet he goes out to recess and remembers complex football plays. The abilities are there. The challenge is to teach the children to develop and use these abilities in school tasks. Today, notice the skills and abilities children have but aren't yet using in school. Make a list of the skills you notice and think where these skills could be used in school. Develop a plan to help your students begin to use these skills in their schoolwork.

Friday—Beliefs About Intentions

Children, like all of us, intend well. Yet often there is a difference, sometimes large, between what children intend and the result of their actions. They are doing the best they can with the knowledge and the choices they have. Even very strange behavior makes sense when we understand what a person's thoughts are. For example, a child may tease or hit another child in an attempt to make friends, or a child may get poor grades in order to fit in with a peer group.

Knowing children intend well does not excuse their behavior. It is a starting place for helping them develop more appropriate choices. Today, when faced with a child's inappropriate behavior, remember he has a positive intent. Help him develop more appropriate behavior.

I create my own self-fulfilling prophecy.

Week of _____

MONDAY	My beliefs	At the end of the year, my class will:
TUESDAY	"Troublemakers"	These children will be responsible and capable students 1. 2. 3. 4.
WEDNESDAY	Image—children want to learn	What I noticed that shows me that my students want to learn 1. 2. 3. 4.
THURSDAY	Everything is there!	Children's hidden skills
FRIDAY	Positive intention	Positive intentions I've noticed 1. 2. 3. 4.

WEEK 3

"Success Breeds Success"

What you focus on is what you'll get!

Monday—Success Folder

Start a week long success folder. Fold a 12" x 18" sheet of paper. Inside, write days of the week with spaces to write successes. Encourage the children to collect papers they were successful at. On the cover, let them write "I am Successful" or another phrase of their choice and then decorate the cover.

Tuesday—Brag Time

Have a Brag Time. Recount successes of your own and of children in the class to get things started. Let the children know it's OK to brag. Ask the children to tell of successes. Encourage them to appreciate the successes of others. **There is enough room in the world for everyone to be successful. When other people are successful, it makes a better world for you to be in and to be successful in.**

Wednesday—Success of Others

Encourage children to notice and comment on the successes of others. Practice accepting compliments and saying "thank you." (It may also be necessary to help the children recognize and stop using put-downs. A good book for this is *I Am Loveable and Capable*.)

Thursday—Success Posters

Make success poster for the classroom of their room at home.

Friday—Success Books for the Year

Make a year-long success book. If children are too young to write, let them draw pictures of their successes. Have them begin by including any past successes that are important to them. The children decide what to include. The success books may be kept private or shared.

(P.S. Make a success book for yourself, too!)

Your own ideas . . .

Relax and dip into your own creative pool for ways to use the idea, "success breeds success."

I did this...   And I
did this...

Week of _____

		My own ideas	My Successes
MONDAY	Success Folder		
	Time_____		
TUESDAY	Brag Time		
	Time_____		
WEDNESDAY	Compliment Others		
	Time_____		
THURSDAY	Success Posters		
	Time_____		
FRIDAY	Success Books		
	Time_____		

Write the ideas here **and** in your daily plan book.

I recognize my own success and the success of others.

WEEK 4

Have A Class of A+ Students

Children will become what they act like. Teach them to act like A+ students!

Monday—Act Like An A+ Student

Discuss how an A+ student acts. Include ideas such as turning in work on time, getting along with others, how he acts toward the teacher, paying attention, answering questions, where and when he completes homework.

Tell your students they can act as if they are A+ students as much of the time as they want to, since they are only pretending. Then notice their successes. You know how you're sometimes ready to pounce on the next student who talks out loud and really make an example of them? Well, be ready to "pounce" on your students when they change to more successful behavior. Let them know, in an appropriate way, that you notice they are succeeding.

Tell them to gather pictures of their concept of an A+ student for a collage they will make tomorrow.

Tuesday—Treasure Map For A+ Behavior

Make a treasure map of an A+ student. Each student makes a collage-type poster of how he will be as an A+ student. It should include all things necessary for him to be an A+ student. It can take the form of an actual treasure map or be a collage or design with the A+ student in the middle and all things necessary arranged around the outside. Any design that is meaningful to the student will be fine. The student may use pictures cut from magazines or draw pictures.

Then the child puts the Treasure Map in a special place of his own choice to refer to and think on daily—his own treasure map to success!

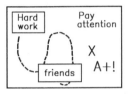
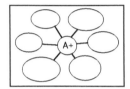

Wednesday—Create An A+ Sanctuary

Tell the children what a sanctuary is—a sacred place where people are safe from outside evil forces. Then tell the children to relax and imagine themselves sitting in a safe, comfortable place—a place they've been or a new one they've created. Make sure they are safe—add walls or guards. Then imagine the tools they will want to have to be able to do whatever they want successfully, to be A+. Include a computer, a library of all the books they have read, a spelling machine, a typewriter, etc., and super heros to give them courage or to make them safe in their dreams. Let them spend some time there, imagining. Then as you direct them to return to the classroom, tell them they may return to their sanctuary any time they choose, to feel safe, get help, or use their imagination.

Thursday—Guessing Game

Teach the children to use their own abilities in guessing. Play a game of guessing—use what you have around you. How many desks in the room? Guess, then count. How many boys? How many girls? What time is it? etc. The children will be amazed at how close they come! Children often disregard their own correct "guesses" and don't offer information for fear of being incorrect. Teach them to trust their hunches—trust themselves, and they'll be more willing to participate in class. Be sure to treat their guesses with respect even when they are incorrect. Their guesses will improve. Encourage them to play the guessing game all day long with insignificant things—how many cracks in the sidewalk, how many traffic lights to the store, what Mom will cook for dinner, etc. Notice their new found confidence and enjoy it!

Help your students transfer this skill of guessing into their schoolwork. When a child says, "I don't know," ask him to guess. Some children, who think they need to be perfect, are so afraid of giving a wrong answer they say they don't know. This is true, they don't KNOW. They are not certain. Telling them to guess frees them to try without becoming identified with the answer and the consequences of it being right or wrong,

thinking they are good if the answer is correct, and they are bad if the answer is wrong.

As the children practice guessing and become more skilled at it, their confidence will increase. Be sure to tell them you don't know everything and let them know when you are guessing, too.

Friday—Self Evaluation

Have the children evaluate their own work today and grade their own papers. Some children will be harder on themselves than you would. Help them to relax their standards and appreciate their work. Others will overestimate their work. Help them to seen their achievement honestly and the improvement needed. For those who are unable to form a judgement, relying only on others to tell them how they did, encourage them to take a chance and guess a grade. Do this every so often to help the children acquire the skill of accurate self-evaluation.

Great!   Wonderful!   Super

Splendid

Fantastic

Very Good   100%

A+

Excellent!

Good!   Yea!

Week of _____

		Review	My own successes this week
MONDAY	Discussion: How an A+ student acts. Tell them to gather pictures. Time_____	Make weekly Success Folder	
TUESDAY	Treasure Map Time_____	Camera Game	
WEDNESDAY	Sanctuary Time_____	Brag Time	
THURSDAY	Guessing Game Time_____	Praise and compliment others—remind the kids to do it at the beginning of the day. Then notice and reinforce it.	
FRIDAY	Evaluate own work All day		

I act like an A+ teacher.

WEEK 5

Following Directions

Being able to comprehend and follow directions leads children to become A+ students and do well at tasks in life. Before children can follow directions, they must (1) be aware that directions are being given, (2) comprehend the directions, and (3) remember them.

Monday—Attention To Directions Game

Teach children to pay close attention when you are giving directions. Give them a signal such as, "This is what you are going to do." Teach them several signals or cue phrases that other teachers might use. Change the tone of your voice or stand in a certain way. Make a game of who can notice first that you are going to give directions and have the "winner" be the one who sits up looking attentive and ready to listen. Play this game often and incorporate in into your daily routine.

Tuesday—Directions Games

Get their attention. Give clear directions on how you want them to play the game.

The teacher gives oral directions, such as, "John, pick up your pencil, go to the door, open it, sharpen your pencil, and return to your seat." The directions are given completely before the students act. Give as many directions as they will be able to remember and then add one more, to give them a chance to increase their abilities. The directions must be followed in the sequence they were given in order to be correct. Variations: directions may be given to the class as a whole (e.g., get out your spelling book, put your pencil on top of it, and stand up). As the children understand how to play the game, some children may be allowed to give directions.

Wednesday—Verbal Directions in Pairs

Get their attention and explain the game. The students will be in pairs, facing each other across a desk with a barrier between them, so A can't see what B is writing. B draws a simple geometric design on paper in front of him and gives **oral directions only** to A, telling him how to reproduce the design B has drawn. B may use words like left, right, curved, straight, up, down, etc., but may not use gestures. A draws from B's directions. B may watch what A draws in order to modify the directions. Compare designs when A is finished drawing . Then let A draw a design and give directions to B. As a group, discuss what worked, what was difficult, etc.

Note: If this is too difficult for your students, have them do Tuesday's game in pairs and discuss "what is important in giving directions."

Thursday—Written Directions

Teach your students to become independent in following written directions in their books, workbooks, and on dittoes. For a class lesson today, go through all their books and workbooks, one at a time, pointing out where the directions are. Show them the cues that the authors have placed in their books to indicate where the directions are. The cues will be words, numbers, stars, bold face type, colored letters, etc. After they have learned how directions are presented in their books, have them turn to a specific page and quickly find the directions. Then teach the children to look for the key words (usually write, read, draw, color, compare, design, describe, etc.). Have them underline the key words if it is a ditto or workbook they can write in. Turn to a new page and have them tell you what they are to do on that page by using only the key words. Be sure to go through all their books so they will transfer this newly learned skill to all subject areas. Discuss other places also where they will be given written directions (instructions for building models, instructions for food preparation on packages, recipes, and games, etc.).

Remind the children daily to look for cues to tell them where directions are and look for the key words in directions until it becomes a habit for them.

Friday—Written Directions in Pairs

Give them a ditto sheet or board assignment of directions to follow. For example:

1. write your name on the bottom left corner of the paper;
2. draw a house in the middle of the paper;
3. draw a lake to the right of the house. Put six ducks in the lake;
4. draw a path from the house to the bottom right cover of the paper;
5. fold your paper in half.

After they have done this, tell them they can make directions for each other. Then explain the game. The children are in pairs. Person A writes directions that B will carry out while B writes directions that A will carry out. When they are both done writing directions, they exchange papers and carry out the directions that were written for them. Follow up with a discussion of what they learned in this experience. Stress the importance of using key words and writing directions clearly. Children will often be amazed at how others will misunderstand directions that they thought were clear.

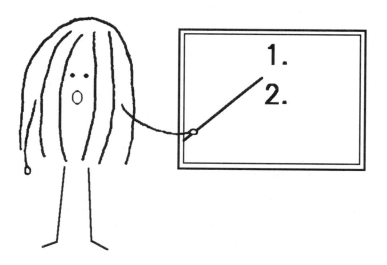

I get the children's attention and give clear directions.

Week of _____

		Review	My Successes
MONDAY	Attention Game	Guessing Game	
	All day	Time_____	
TUESDAY	Directions Game	Songs (use songs that give directions)	Yea!
	Time_____	Time_____	
WEDNESDAY	Verbal Directions in Pairs	Play Simon Says	Super
	Time_____	Time_____	
THURSDAY	Written Directions	Sanctuary fantasy— add signal to notice directions.	A+
	Time_____	Time_____	
FRIDAY	Written Directions in Pairs	Write in Success Book	Great!
	Time_____	Time_____	

WEEK 6

The Key to Spelling—Visual Memory

You've been teaching spelling for some weeks now, and probably your students test scores show good results. This week concentrate on teaching the children *how* to spell and watch their scores improve. The basic skills needed are: visual memory of the word and a way to know if it is correct. Phonetic spelling is "phine" for many words; however, in our English language, phonetic spelling leaves out too many words.

As you play these visual memory games, notice where the childrens' eyes search for answers. A person will remember visual images by looking upward, and auditory images by looking sideways toward his ears. If a person is looking sideways for visual images, direct his eyes upward by moving your hand upward in front of him or by telling him to look up to find the pictures. Notice how quickly they can find the answers when they look in the right place.

Visual Searching   Auditory Searching

Monday—Visual Memory

Teach your students to become aware of making and remembering visual images. Play these games.

1. Tell them to remember their room at home. What color is the floor, the bed cover, the wall? Ask them to remember other things they have seen, e.g., the Wookie in Star Wars.
2. Have one student come to the front of the room. Let the others observe him. Have him leave the room and ask the others to describe in detail what he is wearing. Continue this with other children.

3. Tell the children to close their eyes and imagine a red square, a green circle on the right next to it, and a blue triangle next to that. Then ask questions: which is first, third second? Work up to as many shapes as they can be successful with. Play this with shapes, numbers, letters, words, etc.

Tuesday—Color Game for Visual Memory

Strengthen your students' visual memory skills by playing the Color Game with them. Students are used to remembering letters and numbers and have devised little tricks to help them. In remembering something new, like the sequence of colored stars, they will have to rely more on visual imaging alone, thereby strengthening their skill. After they have increased their visual memory skill, show them how they can use their new, good memory in spelling. Play the game using colored letters, then letters that form words. Finally, teach them to see letter groups as a unit so they can "picture" longer words.

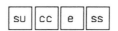

It will take many days of repetition for students to increase their visual memory skill, and still more days of practice using the skill with their spelling words before they have successfully transferred the learned skill to spelling. Remember that you can also teach them to transfer this skill to remembering math facts, location of countries on maps, and many more visual memory tasks.

Have them spell product names (Tide, Pepsi, Ivory, Xerox, Cherios...), words they may have seen on signs (Stop, Speed, Curve) and clothing labels (GUESS, Levis, Adidas), or words on their hats or t-shirts. Notice words in your classroom, walk over to them, cover them up, and ask the class to remember how to spell them (October, Monday, Menu, etc.).

Materials: Flash cards with stars drawn on the. The stars are alike, but each is a different color. Method: Hold up 3 (or more) cards. Remove them. Ask the children which came second, first, etc. Show it again if they miss. Do this in a large group or have the children make their own set and play with each other. Encourage them to use as many cards as they can remember.

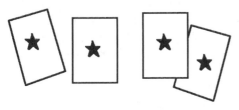

Wednesday—Memory Bank of Spelling Words

Children already know how to spell many words. Point out to them how many words they already know. Then get out their reading book and read them a sentence or paragraph, telling them to write it from memory as you read. Then let them check what they have written against their books. They will be amazed at how many words they have learned to spell by reading. Imagine how many they will learn by the end of the year.

Thursday—Proofreading

Some children will continually misspell small words—or spell them right one time and incorrectly the next time. They need a strategy to know if words are spelled right. Tell them to look at the written word and check with their visual image of the word to see if they are the same. Many people get a feeling that tells them the word is right or wrong. Give them practice to develop their own proofreading strategy. Pair them up in competition. Each child writes a sentence or story and

gives it to the other child who proofreads it. The proofreader circles misspelled words. Scoring: every correctly circled word is one point. Every miscircled work is one point off. Every misspelled word uncircled is one point off. The child with the highest score wins.

Friday—Spelling Backwards for Visual Memory

If students are asked to spell a word backwards, or reverse the order of numbers given, they will have to find a way to hold the image in their mind while they reverse it. The skill of holding the image is visual memory.

Begin the game by asking the class to reverse the order of a number, i.e., what is 368 backwards? Ask them to write their number but not to write the number you said first. Give them the correct answer and have them signal you if they got it correct by raising their hand. Proceed to longer numbers and simple words, such as "What is C-A-T backwards?"

Group the class according to how many digits or letters they can reverse. Let the more proficient players pair off and play the game with someone of like skill while you work with the ones who are having difficulty. Teach them to put the letters or numbers in their minds one at a time so they can see them. Then ask them to read backwards. Let them play the game with spelling words that are an appropriate length. If they can spell the word backward, they will be able to spell it forward.

Resources

—The book *Put Your Mother On the Ceiling* has visual imagery exercises that are read aloud by the teacher.
—*Spelling Strategy* and *Spelling Gallery*. Software games helpful in building the skill of detecting incorrectly spelled words.
—*Visual Imagery* audio tapes—*Mini Mind Benders*. The children are told "word pictures" and then asked to draw them.

Week of _____

MONDAY	Visual imagery	Read a story to the children, telling them to imagine a movie of the story as they listen.
	Time: _____	
TUESDAY	Color Game	In Social Studies, have the students close their eyes while you take them on a fantasy trip to the time or place you are studying.
	Time: _____	
WEDNESDAY	Memory Bank	Creative writing—discuss photographic memory. Then have the children write what they would do if they had that skill.
	Time: _____	
THURSDAY	Proofread	In pairs, according to math ability, the children take turns giving each other math problems to work in their heads.
	Time: _____	
FRIDAY	Spelling Backwards	Have them list the steps in making a peanut butter sandwich.
	Time: _____	

I teach children HOW to learn.

WEEK 7

Auditory Memory

Children are often called upon to "memorize." While this is basically an auditory memory activity, it is easier to memorize when they make visual images of the material they are memorizing. As your students do these and other memorizing tasks, encourage them to use their visual imagery and memory skills.

Go slowly at first, giving them time to create the image. Say the number, letter, or word and tell them to imagine it or see it in their mind's eye. Then say the next symbol and tell them to imagine it to the right of the first one. Have them give you a signal, such as raising a finger, to let you know they have created the image and are ready for the next one. Then have them tell you what they "see." Watch their eyes. Tell them to look at the image they created as they "read" the symbols. If they are using the visual image, tell them to look for the pictures they made, or direct their eyes upward with a sweep of your arm.

Monday—Auditory Discrimination and Memory

Sam-ham

boy-toy

salt-salt

base-bake

To memorize accurately, children must be able to first discriminate the sounds they hear. This game is for training as well as testing. The teacher says two words or phrases (depending on the students' ability level), and the students indicate whether they are the same or different by writing on paper (S for same, D for different or by a hand signal).

Tuesday—Tape Recorder Game for Auditory Memory

The children will act as tape recorders. You will say a sequence of numbers, letters or words and the children will repeat them accurately. When they know the game, let them play in pairs. Halfway through, tell them to now act as video recorders by making a visual image of the sequence of words or letters they are remembering. Later discuss whether the visual image helped them.

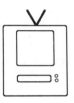

Wednesday—Auditory—Memory Aids

This is a technique for remembering lists of words in order. It uses visual imagery to aid remembering. A list of memory aids is permanently memorized. Then any other list of words may be remembered by connecting the new list to the old. An example would be as follows: if the memory aid for one is bun and the first word on the new list is apples, create a visual image of an apple in a bun. Then apple will be remembered as #1 on the list. Many different new lists can be attached to the memory aid list.

This type of exercise is useful because we are only able to remember about seven items without some technique like this. How many items can you remember when you go to the store? And at what point do you make a list? This technique allows us to remember many more items.

First of all, memorize these "memory aids." Notice that the aids rhyme with the number.

1. bun
2. shoe
3. tree
4. door
5. hive

6. sticks
7. heaven
8. gate
9. dine
10. den

To memorize these aids, discuss the meaning of each word and create visual images for the word. Choose other words if the class desires. Notice the similarity to "One, Two, Button My Shoe."

When they have memorized the aids, give them a list of words to memorize and practice on, e.g., hat, cat, bat, sat, fat, etc. Anything will work. You can even have them create the list of words to memorize. Create a visual image of the first word including the memory aid, e.g., hat—a hat in a bun, cat—a cat in a shoe, bat—a bat in a tree, and so on.

The more elaborate or outrageous the picture, the more likely they are to remember. When they have learned this technique, give them content from their curriculum to practice on, i.e., states, times tables, names, etc.

Thursday—Memorize Poems

Each student chooses some written work to memorize. Teach them to memorize this by choosing an important word or idea from each line, writing it as a cue for the line. Then make a visual image of the written cues and practice until the piece is memorized. Use the memory technique from yesterday to memorize the sequence of cue words.

Choose a date in the near future (Friday?) for the children to present a "concert" of their memorized pieces. If the children are too young, do this as a group and use pictures instead of words.

Friday—Secretary Game—Short Term Auditory Memory

Have the children pair up. It is helpful if they choose partners of the same writing ability. They act as secretary for each other in a creative writing project. One creates aloud while the other one writes. The one who is writing gets practice in holding words in their mind while spelling and writing—and he has a friend to help him remember.

I teach children HOW to learn and then give them practice.

Week of _____

		Visual memory review	Songs to sing this week
MONDAY	Auditory Discrimination		
	Time_____	Time_____	
TUESDAY	Tape Recorder Game	Color Game	
	Time_____	Time_____	
WEDNESDAY	Memory Aids	Practice memory aids in content area area_____	
	Time_____	Time_____	
THURSDAY	Memorize poems or prose	Proofreading Game	
	Time_____	Time_____	
FRIDAY	Secretary or Dictaphone Game	Concert of memorized works	
	Time_____	Time_____	

WEEK 8

Your View of the World

We are continuously responding to everything going on inside our minds as well as what we sense around us. However, we are only **aware** of what we choose to pay attention to, or what our attention is drawn to. Children will learn what we bring to their awareness (good or bad!) and these learnings will form the basis of their belief system.

Monday—Attention—Creating Views

Get their attention! If a child is "inside," he won't receive what is "outside"—namely the lesson. Bring your students out of their daydream or rerun of past events by involving them in what you are doing.

Choose any lesson you plan to teach today. Plan to vary your activities to include auditory, visual, and kinesthetic experiences. If you notice a student's attention wandering, attract him back by drawing his attention to a picture or diagram, asking him a question, or assigning an activity.

Tuesday—People Have Different Views

People create their own "illusion" of the real world from the interaction of their internal thinking and their sensing of the outside world. Everybody's illusion is different! Some of the strange things people do seem to make sense when we understand their view of the world.

Ask the children several questions on which you think they will have widely differing opinions.

How should parents raise children? What do you think of school? Math? Reading? Recess? etc. Use what will stimulate your group. Help them to notice that people think differently. Chart different views of one issue on the chalkboard.

Wednesday—Interviews—Discovering A Person's View

Discuss questions the children could ask another person in order to find out how that person interprets the world. Talk to them about privacy and invasion of privacy. Help them to be tactful. (Optional: have them pair up with another child they think is different from them and get to know how the other person thinks and views the world.) Homework: ask the children to choose someone they know of a different age, sex, or lifestyle and ask that person to tell them about their life.

Thursday—Inside Another's View—What It's Like To Be...

Ask the children to choose an animal, plant, or object, and imagine what it would be like to be that. Guide them in their fantasy by asking such questions as, Where are you? What do you feel inside? Can you move or talk? If you eat, what does it taste like? What do people do with you? Then have them draw a picture and/or write what it is like to be that other thing. Have the students show their work and discuss it.

Friday—Recreating Your View of the World

It's useful to act as though our view of the world is true, and then change it when we get new information. This is one way to learn. (Problems start when people cling to their illusion in the face of contradictory information.) Explain this. Then ask the children to think of a time when they were younger and learned from a mistake or corrected a misconception—or when they noticed someone else learning this way. Let them share these stories.

Resources

Frogs into Princes. Richard Bandler, Real People Press, Box F, Moab, Utah 84532.

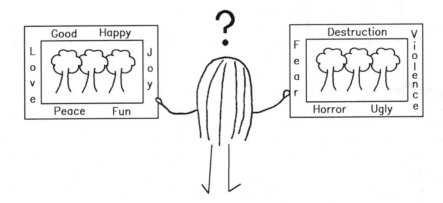

We don't have to change the world...we can change our view of the world.

Week of _____

MONDAY	Attention	These things worked in keeping children's attention:
TUESDAY	People are different	Questions to use in discussion:
WEDNESDAY	Interviews	You do it too! "Interview" someone you work with today.
THURSDAY	"What it's like to be..."	What it's like to be a student...
FRIDAY	Recreating A View	Illusions I have known (and let go...)

WEEK 9

How We Think—Perception

Thinking is talking to yourself, making pictures, feeling, smelling and tasting—inside your mind. These are the same sense areas you use to bring in information from the outside world. We can only pay attention, at any one time, to about seven pieces of information out of all the information we are sensing and are thinking. We can choose what we pay attention to.

Monday—Perception—Inside or Outside?

1. Ask the children to pay attention to the sights, sounds, smells, touches, and tastes around them. Do this silently for a minute or two and then report what they noticed.

2. Ask the children to pay attention to the sights, sounds, etc. inside their minds. Again, do this quietly for a few minutes and then report in a group discussion.

3. Ask the children to be silent for another minute or two and just notice whether they are paying attention to the inside or the outside. Discuss.

Do they switch back and forth quickly, or do they stay with one for a while?

Tuesday—Perception—Awareness

Tell the children you are going to help them discover what they pay attention to in their minds. Have them make a chart they will use to count the number of times they think in pictures, words, and feelings. Tell them to just notice their thoughts, mark the appropriate column, and notice again. Do this silently for a few minutes. Discussion: some people think mostly in one area—some people think in all areas. Most people think in one area for some things and another area for others.

Wednesday—Discover Signal Words

We can tell how people think by the words they choose. People who use words like "you see" and "colorful" are thinking in pictures. People who use words like "that sounds good" and "harmonize" are thinking in sounds. People who think in feelings will use words like "I feel" and "that's rough." And, when people think in smells or tastes, they will use words like "stinky" or "sweet." After explaining this to the children, search with them for words that signal thinking in these areas. Make a permanent chart of their lists for future use.

See	Hear	Feel
II	III	II

Visual	Auditory	Kinesthetic	Smell/Taste
clear	hear	feel	bitter
focus	amplify	warm	salty
image	tune	handle	fragrant
insight	sound	grasp	smell
view	saying	tight	stale
appear	listen	smooth	taste
vague	talk	rough	sweet
flash	sounding board	in touch	fresh
perspective	scream	sore	sour
bright	shout	sharp	
show	tone	cutting	
obvious	in other words	cold	

Thursday—Notice Signal Words

Ask if any of the children noticed people using signals words from the chart. Discuss. To stimulate noticing, ask them to write three sentences about something they like or dislike, telling why. Then look for signal words in their writing. Or in a group, ask someone to tell about something they like or dislike, as the rest of the group notices signal words.

Friday—Practice Using Signal Words

Choose a thinking area (seeing, feeling, etc.) and describe a recent event using mostly words from the one area. Ask the class to guess which area you were using. Then choose another area and describe the same event. Have them guess again. When they understand how the game works, let them choose an area and talk before the group, or play in groups of three, alternating speakers and guessers.

Resources

The Centering Book
The Second Centering Book
Left Handed Teaching

I appreciate each person's unique way of sensing the world and thinking.

Week of _____

MONDAY   Inside or Outside?   Exercises for YOU to do:

                                            Take three minutes to notice—Do I
                                            prefer inside or outside?

                  Time_____

TUESDAY   Awareness   Take 3 min. to notice:

See	Hear	Feel

                  Time_____

WEDNESDAY   Discover   Listen to one person—which signal words
                  Signal Words   do they prefer?

                  Time_____

THURSDAY   Notice Signal   Listen to another person—which signal
                  Words   words do they prefer?

                  Time_____

FRIDAY   Use Signal Words   The signal words I use most are:

                  Time_____

WEEK 10

Noticing How Others Think

The signal words people choose often indicate the main way they will process the information they take in—usually auditory, visual, or kinesthetic. It is easier for people who "think" the same way to understand each other. Notice for yourself how much easier it is to understand people who use words that fit your way of thinking. In your lessons, use and teach **all** ways of thinking to reach **all** students.

Monday—Visual Thinking

Visual thinkers can think of many things at once. They think in pictures. Pictures represent ideas. They can picture many ideas simultaneously and move those pictures around to think—put them in sequence, add more pictures, put two together to make a new one, change a picture, etc. Possibilities are endless. Children who do well with abstract ideas, math, word recognition, spelling, reasoning, problem solving, social perception, and nonverbal communication are likely to be good visual thinkers. Use these same subject areas to teach visual thinking. Represent ideas with pictures. Use pictures instead of words to show the change in something. Use visual signal words. For example, tell your students you will "show" them how England "looked" to the colonists. Draw a chalkboard picture of a large, controlling, parental figure looking down at a small child. Another example is to diagram the water cycle as you explain it. Choose one area today to begin teaching using visual thinking.

Tuesday—Auditory Thinking

Auditory thinking is linear—in a line—one idea follows another. Auditory thinkers think of only one idea at a time and then move on to the next one. This is slower, more thorough thinking. Children who do well at reading comprehension, following directions, expressive writing, verbal expression, and verbal communication are likely to be good auditory thinkers. Use these same areas to teach auditory thinking. Help them to slow down and consider one idea at a time. Stress comprehension, following directions, reasoning. Choose an area today to teach and use auditory thinking.

Wednesday—Kinesthetic Thinking

Kinesthetic thinkers trust their feelings, hunches, intuitions. They "know" something rather than "think it through." They can get involved with what they are doing and concentrate amid distractions. They express their feelings as they express themselves through art, writing, etc. Help your students gain trust in their guesses and hunches. Ask questions and have discussions where there is no right answer, where guesses and options are valid. Choose an area today and adapt it to include kinesthetic thinking.

Thursday—Noticing Preferred Mode of Thinking in Our Students

Notice which way of thinking your children prefer by the words they use. Review common signal words in the last lesson. As you notice a child's preference, note his name here.

Auditory	Visual	Kinesthetic

Ah!

Now let me see...

I notice nonverbal cues.

Friday—Noticing Eyes—Noticing Thinking

When children ponder, the position of their eyes may also indicate their way of thinking. When they ponder visually they will usually look up. (This does not necessarily mean they are day-dreaming.) When they look sideways or down to their left, they may be pondering auditorily. When they are looking down to the right, or they are moving their body around, they may be doing kinesthetic thinking. Generally, people's eyes will rapidly move around as they switch from one mode of thinking to another. Individual patterns will develop for different types of thinking.

When you notice children pondering, it may mean they are processing the information you gave them. Give them time to complete this process. When they "come back out," continue on.

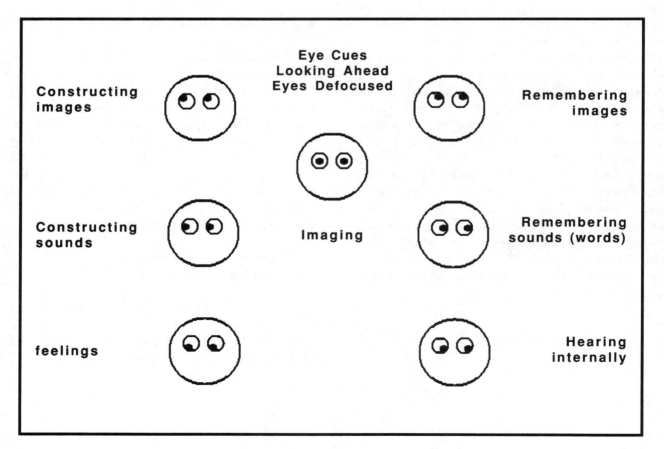

Eye Cues
Looking Ahead
Eyes Defocused

Constructing images

Remembering images

Constructing sounds

Imaging

Remembering sounds (words)

feelings

Hearing internally

Week of _____

MONDAY	Visual imagery	Subject area: I will: Time: _____
TUESDAY	Auditory Thinking	Subject area: I will: Time: _____
WEDNESDAY	Kinesthetic Thinking	Subject area: I will: Time: _____
THURSDAY	Noticing Words	In the staff room or on a TV interview show, notice a person's preferred way of thinking by listening to their signal words. I discovered:
FRIDAY	Noticing Eyes	In the staff room or on a TV interview show, notice a person's preferred way of thinking by looking at their eyes as they ponder. I discovered:

I notice how other people think.

WEEK 11

Getting Through To People

Most people choose one sensory area as the main way in which they take in information. As a teacher, you have probably developed one favorite mode of teaching. Expand that to reach all children: those who need to "see" what you are saying, those who have to "hear" you, and those who want to "understand" you.

Monday—Getting Through Visually

Use specific facial expressions, drawings, pictures, charts, and the chalkboard for visual children. Use an uncluttered chalkboard and emphasize main points by writing key words. Visual children will respond to our facial expressions for reward or punishment. Think of how you can encourage a child with a smile!

Today, be aware of how you can add to your lessons visually. Change one thing you do to include more visual teaching.

Tuesday—Getting Through Auditorily

Not only what you say, but how you say it will have great impact on auditory children. Your voice tone can be used to great effect. Experiment with your voice tone—tones of reprimand, encouragement, excitement, awe, etc. You can make an otherwise dull lesson very exciting (and keep the attention of your auditory students) by using your voice. Experiment with your rate of speech, speeding up, slowing down—meeting the rate of speech of your students and then gradually changing to a slower rate for learning. Be aware of your voice today. Choose one thing you will

change or experiment with. Even reading a story with new voice is a start.

Wednesday—Getting Through Kinesthetically

Kinesthetic children are concerned with how they are feeling and with their emotions. These are the children who must be comfortable to pay attention. They are concerned with the feelings or emotions of the characters they read about. They can get totally involved and enthusiastic or they can get bored and wiggle a lot. They want to feel interested and involved with what they are doing. They learn well in games, from exciting stories, when they get to write on the chalkboard or perform an experiment. Rather than always try to be interesting enough to excite them to learn, give them a lesson where they can participate, involving and exciting themselves. Using your curriculum, plan a lesson for today that will allow children to participate.

Thursday—Noticing How To Get Through

The preferred way to taking in information can be detected by noticing where a child first looks when asked a general question (one that does not require a specific hearing, seeing, or feeling answer). If a child first looks up, he is "looking" for the answer. If a child moves his eyes to the side or down left, he is trying to "hear" the answer. If he looks down right or wiggles, he is feeling for the answer. As you are with your children today, notice their preferred way of taking in information and write some of their names here.

Auditory   Visual   Kinesthetic

_____

_____

_____

_____

The primary way a person takes in information may be in a different mode from the way he processes it. For example, a person may "see" something and then have "feelings" about it. Notice his eyes go up and then down right. Since we are not always aware of what we are taking in, we may have feelings or thoughts and not be aware of how we got them. As we become more aware of where our thoughts originate, we have more choices. For instance, we can change our pictures or what we tell ourselves, and our feelings change.

Friday—Practicing Getting Through

As you are teaching today and you notice a child not paying attention, attract his attention by altering your voice or gestures, or letting him participate in some way. Write down what happened.

I teach to reach all children.

Week of _____

MONDAY	Visual Lesson	What I will do to increase visual teaching
	Time: _____	
TUESDAY	Auditory Lesson	What I will do to increase auditory teaching
	Time: _____	
WEDNESDAY	Kinesthetic Lesson	What I will do to increase kinesthetic involvement
	Time: _____	
THURSDAY	Noticing the preferred mode of children	In the staff room, ask another person some questions—notice their eyes—where do they first search for the answer?
	Time: _____	
FRIDAY	Attracting attention	These things help keep my students' attention:
	Time: _____	

WEEK 12

Thanksgiving

We get more of what we're thankful for!

By paying more attention to what we are thankful for, we actually help to create more of it for ourselves.

Monday—Say "Thank You"

Begin by saying thank you. Let others know what you appreciate and how it helped you or what you enjoyed about it. The children may begin thanking others just from your model. Tell them the secret of how to get more of what you want: by being thankful for it **as if** you already had it!

Tuesday—Thankful book

Lead a discussion of what we can be thankful for. Then have the children make their own thankful book or list.

Wednesday—Future Thankful Book

By acting as though we already have what we want, and by being thankful for it, our minds will help us to achieve it. Have the children create a future thankful book including material objects, personal achievements, friends, living conditions etc. Encourage them to be as specific as possible—describe in detail, draw pictures, etc.

Thanks!

We get more of what we're thankful for!

Week of _____

MONDAY	Say "Thank you"	My Thankful List:
TUESDAY	Thankful List or Book	
WEDNESDAY	Future Thankful book or list	

Make a Future Thankful List of what you would like to accomplish in
your classroom during the rest of the school year. Be specific!

1.

2.

3.

4.

5.

WEEK 13

Getting Correct Answers

After we have taken in information and processed it (or thought about it), the information is stored in our minds until we recall it. We may recall it to answer a question, compare one piece of information with another, enjoy a memory, feel an emotion, etc. The recall of the image, sound, feeling, taste, or smell is triggered by another image, sound, feeling, taste, and/or smell. Try an experiment. Think of a chocolate chip cookie. Then notice your thoughts as they move from one idea to another, each one triggered by the one before. We move from sensing things in our environment to our thoughts and back again—our minds constantly processing our experience—whether we are aware of it or not. Until I mentioned it, you were probably not aware of the feeling of your body against your chair. To be able to remember specific things, we must be able to recall and be aware of what we are looking for. You may have had the experience of trying to remember a word that was "on the tip of your tongue." It was there and you could feel it, but you couldn't say it.

Monday—Teach To Recall Answers

How we put information in our minds has a lot to do with how readily we are able to retrieve it. If we put it in by feeling, seeing, hearing, tasting, **and** smelling it—that is, by fully experiencing it— we have a much better change of retrieving it. Also, we have learned to tune out parts of our environment—selectively. For example, Johnny didn't hear Mom tell him to take out the trash, yet he heard his brother open the cookie jar! We are not likely to retrieve tuned out information.

To be sure our students learn and are able to retrieve information, we need to get their full attention and to teach them in all sensory areas— auditory, visual, and kinesthetic.

Today, notice your teaching procedures. Are you teaching in all sense areas? Do you have their full attention? Are your students involved?

Tuesday—Contextualize Questions And Answers

Amy knew that 2 + 2 = 4, but she didn't realize that a story problem about Bobby giving away half of his 4 toys cars had anything to do with it. In order to teach something, we often isolate it from the context in which it is usually found. This is fine, but it is important to contextualize the skill once it is learned, to put it back into the setting where it will be useful. Make the triggers that we retrieve the information like the "real world." So when Amy gives Susie two of her four jawbreakers, Amy know she will have two left.

Choose one lesson today. Contextualize the skill taught.

Wednesday—Understanding the Question Before Answering

In order to answer a question, or to retrieve learned information, we have to know what we are looking for. What is the question anyway? Teach your students to thoroughly understand a question before answering it. Prepare a list of questions about one of today's lessons. Ask the questions, and one by one have students tell you in their own words what the question is. Use all types of questions—detail, comparison, inference, defining, etc. Don't be concerned with answers at this point. Develop your students' ability to understand questions first.

Thursday—Guessing Answers

Our minds are marvelous. How often have you heard a question, and, when you heard someone else answer, realized you had thought of it but didn't dare say it because you might be wrong? Often that first answer that flashes across our minds is right—but we think it away —"oh, that's not right," "I can't say that," etc.

Make your classroom a safe place for students to try that first guess. Help them to become better and better guessers. Structure your lessons so you ask questions that have guesses as the answer! Interrupt a story with, "What could happen next?" All guesses are valid because your students couldn't know. Before you teach a lesson about whales, ask your students to guess what a whale might eat, how it raises its young, etc. Respect their guesses. As your students have more experience with guessing, they'll get better and better. Encourage reluctant guessers, and praise them for trying. During "guessing practice", don't tell if the guesses are correct. Let the students themselves find out in the following reading or lecture etc. Incidentally, they will become more skilled at discovering answers.

Have your first guessing practice today. Choose some area of content you can successfully apply this principle to.

Friday—Checking Answers

Now that you've got them guessing, teach them a strategy to know if their guess is correct. Do it visually, i.e., fit that guess into the total picture and see if it looks right. Or, for the auditory student, "put in the missing word and listen to how it sounds." The kinesthetic check might be "Does it feel right?" We may not be aware of exactly how we know that we know—but we do know. Tell your students they do indeed have a checking mechanism. (Notice your students' eye movement response to the question, "How do you know?" This will display their way of knowing.) Give them a chance to practice, on teacher prepared and teacher answered worksheets. Include math errors, misspelled words, proofreading, fill in the blanks, and whatever else might be appropriate. Include several errors in each area. Have them "check" your work. Afterwards, discuss the various types of checking strategies your students used.

I encourage my students to respond.

Week of _____

MONDAY   Teach in all senses   I noticed:

                                               I will:

TUESDAY   Contextualize   Isolated skills I want to contextualize:

                    Lesson_____

                    Time_____

WEDNESDAY   Understanding   Review any written directions today—
                    questions   be sure all children know what to do.

                    Time_____

THURSDAY   Guessing practice   I can use guessing in these areas:

                    Time_____

FRIDAY   Checking strategy   My checking strategy:

                    Time_____

WEEK 14

Be A Super Problem Solver

We all have problems—it's how we treat them that matters.

Monday—Wise Denial of Problems

Many **problems** are simply worries in disguise—and worrying never solved anything. The Worry Can technique stops needless worry. We all like to worry sometimes—so, when you do worry, enjoy it! Set aside an hour a week for the pure pleasure of worry. All week long, save up your worries by writing them down and placing them in a worry can. Then when the work hour comes, get out the can and worry away. You may find that many worries ar solved in the meantime. This will free you up for more productive behavior the rest of the week.

Teach this technique to the kids and let them make a worry can. Cover a can and decorate it. Encourage them to set aside their worry time and begin saving up their worries.

Tuesday—Exchange Problems

Life is full of problems. If you have a problem you don't like, exchange it for another one! The person who has a problem keeping cool on a hot day forgets all about it when he gets hungry. If you have a problem wondering if others like you, think about how you can be a friend to people instead, and your original problem will disappear. It's your life and you can choose whatever problems you want. What you focus on is what you get.

Teach this concept to the children. Provide examples of initial problems from their environment as well as replacement problems. If appropriate, role play situations. Encourage the children to discuss how their feelings change as their problems change.

Wednesday—Reframing Problems

Just as changing a frame on a picture can change our total view of the picture, changing how we look at a situation can change how we feel about it. If I'm unhappy because my students make noise during an activity, I can also think of that noise as an indication that the children are involved and learning. (A quick check will determine if this is, in fact, true.) A day can be partly sunny or partly cloudy, a glass half empty or half full.

Today, choose two pictures (one happy, one gloomy) and show them to your students. Put mats of different colored paper behind each picture and change the colors to show how the frame affects how they feel when they see the picture. Tell them that we put picture frames of thoughts around how we view life. Have them decide the way they want to view the world.

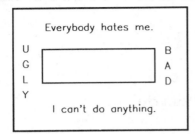

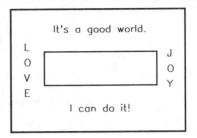

Turn the children loose in their creative process to design a picture from colored paper (their choice of color) that demonstrates how they want to view the world.

Let them hold up their picture frame and view the world through it.

Thursday—Solution Screen for Problems

Imagine a blank movie screen. Put your problem on the screen with all related aspects of the problem. Now imagine another blank screen. This is the solution screen. Notice your first answer that appears. (This is usually the one for you. Don't think it away.) Then in the next few days, when you think of the problem—immediately think of the solution and then let it go.

Sometimes your solution may seem unrelated to the problem, i.e., you think of strawberries for a money problem. This may mean that you should think of something else (such as strawberries) and not try to solve the problem now. Teach this technique to the children and guide them in practicing it.

Friday—Problem Solving

When you have a problem, you have a variety of choices of what to do with it. Here are some:

1. Put it in the Worry Can
2. Exchange it for another problem
3. Reframe it
4. Seek a solution

Review these choices. Then present several sample problems that might be common to the lives of your students. Let them choose how they would want to handle them.

Optional: Graph the choices and indicate which one is chosen for each problem.

Problems
1. _____
2. _____

I choose my own problems and how I react to them.

Week of _____

MONDAY	Worry Can	Worries to put in my can: 1. 2. 3.
	Time_____	
TUESDAY	Exchange Problem	I will exchange _____ _____ problem for _____ _____
	Time_____	
WEDNESDAY	Reframe	My frame for viewing the world
	Time_____	
THURSDAY	Solution Screen	Ask a question My solution screen test your own solution screen
	Time_____	
FRIDAY	Review	Choose a problem What will I do with it?
	Time_____	

WEEK 15

Giving (For The Holiday Season)

Everybody has unique gifts that only he can offer to others. Help the children discover their specialness and what they have to offer in this season of giving.

Monday—The Gift of Time

Only you can give your time to someone else. Time to be together quietly, to play, to share an activity you both enjoy. Think of the people you will spend time with, especially those people for whom it would be a special gift (i.e., grandparents).

Make a book, "How I Spend My Time." Draw a picture and/or write a sentence for each person or group of people you give your time to.

Tuesday—The Gift of Words

Think of those words of affection or praise that have had special meaning to you. You can give those words too. Today, discuss words of affection and appreciation with the children—how it feels to receive and give them. Tell or read the Warm Fuzzy Tale. Practice giving and receiving compliments. Optional: Write a letter telling someone of your affection, appreciation or compliment them.

Wednesday—The Gift of Actions

Ask your students to think of things that people have done for them and how they felt about it. List them. Then discuss and list things they can do for others. Each student can make a plan of action gifts they can give to the people in their lives.

Thursday—Material Gifts

Discuss: You can buy gifts for people, or you can make something that will be one of a kind and especially from you.

Have materials ready for the children to make a card, picture, or something else for someone they care about. Please be prepared to give them more time in the future so they can carry through with projects they may start. Enjoy!

Friday—Gift List

Discuss different types of gifts: time, words, deeds, bought gifts and hand made gifts. Have the children make a Giving Book for the holiday season. On each page make a picture and/or words of them giving the gift they have chosen for a special person.

References

Warm Fuzzy Book

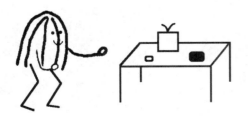

Week of _____

MONDAY	How I spend my time	I will give time to: 1. 2. 3. 4.
	Time: _____	
TUESDAY	Warm Fuzzy Book	Today I will give 3 "warm fuzzies" in words or letters: 1. 2. 3.
	Time: _____	
WEDNESDAY	Discuss and role play	I will offer to help: 1. 2. 3. 4.
	Time: _____	
THURSDAY	Make gifts and cards	My Giving List: 1. 2. 3.
	Time _____	
FRIDAY	Giving Book	1. 2. 3. 4. 5. 6. 7.

I give of myself to other people.

WEEK 16

Change Those Unwanted Habits—Happy New Year!

Happy New Year! This is the time to begin again, to make New Year's Resolutions, to change habits. Habits are wonderful—we couldn't live without them. Habits let us walk, talk, eat, throw a ball, etc. Habits are learned actions that we have practiced until they are automatic. When we **want** a change a habit, we:

1) notice when we are doing the old habit;
2) substitute the new habit;
3) practice until it is automatic.

Monday—Notice Habits

Discuss: Habits can be changed quickly. Choose something you do the same every day—e.g., which shoe you put on first—and **change your habit.**

Do: Every day, when you are getting dressed, PUT THE OTHER SHOE ON FIRST. If you are used to putting on the right shoe, CHANGE and put on the left first. Tell your students that if they forget and then remember later, that is a good time to take  off their shoe and Do It Now. Optional: Practice putting on the other shoe first. Think ahead to tomorrow morning when you will do it again . . . and all the other mornings.

Tuesday—Cancel Habits

Ask how many children put the other shoe on first. Notice. For the ones who didn't do it, let them change shoes now.

Today, begin changing words. The words we use direct our thinking, feeling and behaving. If we change our words, we change our thinking, feeling and behaving. For example, every time you say "hate," say "cancel, cancel . . . love, love, love." Soon not only your words will change, but also your thoughts, feelings and actions.

Discuss this technique. As a class, list negative words and the positive word you will change each to.

Example:
Hate . . . love	poor . . . rich
can't . . . will	bad . . . good
ugly . . . beautiful	

Choose three words to concentrate on and practice. Optional: Teacher use a negative word and invite the children to interrupt with "Cancel, cancel . . . _____, _____, _____." Practice with those three words until the class will spontaneously interrupt. (Giving them the chance to interrupt something "important"  will help them interrupt their own "important" sequences.)

cancel
cancel . . .

Wednesday—Counting Habits

Keeping count of a habit will often be enough to cause a change. Explain this to the class and suggest an experiment. Choose a habit that the group wants to change, i.e., putting others down. Then, on the chalkboard, keep count hourly, of the number of times they use putdowns. Find out if the number decreases as the day goes on. Don't criticize or reprimand, merely count.

Thursday—Have A Perfect Anything Habit

1. Ask how many put on the other shoe first.
2. Use a negative word and notice if they cancel it.
3. Do you want a perfect Mom, teacher, brother, sister, friend, anything?

Step 1. List 25 to 100 things that would make this person perfect.
Step 2. List the same number of things I'd do and be if I had the perfect (Mom, friend, etc.) person.

Do it, be it, and you'll get it!

Friday—Plan A Change in Habits

Ask each child to choose a habit they wish to change and plan how they will accomplish it. In three weeks, you will ask the children how many did it. (Put this on your calendar now.)

I will _____
_____
_____
by _____
date
signed ___

My "New Me" resolution!

Week of _____

MONDAY	Put On The Other Shoe	Tomorrow, I will put on the other shoe first!
	Time: _____	
TUESDAY	Cancel, Cancel...	Negative Words to Positive Words 1. 1. 2. 2. 3. 3. 4. 4.
	Time: _____	
WEDNESDAY	Counting	Try it for yourself! Habit _____ 1st hr. _____ 4th hr. _____ 2nd hr. _____ 5th hr. _____ 3rd hr. _____ What happened?
	Time: _____	
THURSDAY	A Perfect _____	How I'd be if I had a perfect principal (or spouse, friend, child, parent): 1. 2. 3. 4. 5. 6. 7.
	Time: _____	
FRIDAY	Plan a Change	8. 9. 10. 11.
	Time: _____	

WEEK 17

What Do You <u>Really</u> Want?

Many times we are unaware of choosing a goal until we find ourselves pursuing that goal (as in buying something we saw advertised!). By slowing down the goal choosing process, we can help our students (and ourselves) become more aware of what we really want.

Monday—Choose Something to Want

Today, tell your students they really can develop their lives the way they want. Human beings are goal achieving organisms—and, if we don't have goals of our own, we will work to achieve goals that we believe others have for us.

Give your students a blank sheet of paper and tell them it's like their life—they can live it the way they choose. Tell them to pick a goal (or goals, depending on your students). Have them choose what they would like to have, do, or become. If they don't know what to write, ask them if they want to create their own life, or if they want others to write it for them. Either way, it will get written, their life will get lived. Save their goals for tomorrow.

Tuesday—What Would Happen If You Got What You Wanted?

Often what we ask for is not what we really need. We may wish very hard for something, and then once we get it, wish even harder for it to go away. Sometimes the most difficult thing is to ask for something worth having.

Have your students review their goal, asking:

"What would happen if I got what I asked for?" "How would I feel?" "Is this what I really want to have happen?" Once they become more aware of the intent of their desire, they will be more able to choose goals that give them what they really want. To help them discover their intent, ask them to fill in: "I want this (goal) to happen so that _____."

Give them their goal from yesterday, and have them write or draw what the outcome or results would be of having their goal fulfilled. Let them change or revise their goal if they wish.

Wednesday—Be Specific in What You Want

It is important to be able to recognize the fulfillment of our goal when it happens. Some people walk past their goal fulfillment many times before they notice it! Since the way we notice anything is through our senses, it is helpful to describe the goal in specific sense terms.

Ask:
"What would I see?"
"What would I hear?"
"What would I feel?"
"What would I taste and/or smell?"

Have your students describe their goal is specific terms.

Ask them to talk about it to the class or to a partner, have them draw a picture, or act it out. Use whatever is appropriate for your students.

The more specific they are, the more likely they are to get exactly what they want. You can't hit a target you can't see!

 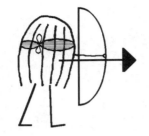

Thursday—Do You Have What You Want Now?

Now that your students have decided what they want to have, do, or become, it's time to take a look at where they are now—what they already have.

Ask them to make a list of what they are grateful for—include people, things, accomplishments, etc.

Then ask them to make another list of qualities, skills, abilities, etc., that they possess. If appropriate, ask them to share things on their list with the group.

Upon evaluation, your students may be surprised to find they already have some of the things they were seeking. They just hadn't recognized what they had.

Tell them to begin thinking how they can use their resources—what they have now—to get what they want.

Friday—Three Ways of Getting What You Want

Have your students list three ways they could achieve their goal. Then have them think of the consequences of doing each of those three ways. ("How would I feel? What might happen? How might others react?") If they discard one option, have them choose another, until they come up with three viable ways to get what they want.

I choose goals that are worth having.

Week of _____

MONDAY	Choose Something to Want:	My goal:
	Time: _____	
TUESDAY	What Is The Outcome?	The outcome of my goal:
	Time: _____	
WEDNESDAY	Be Specific	My goal specifically:
	Time: _____	
THURSDAY	Do I Have It Now?	My abilities:
	Time: _____	
FRIDAY	Three Ways:	Three ways to achieve my goal: 1. 2. 3.
	Time: _____	

WEEK 18

Success In Getting What You Want

Now that your students have chosen and evaluated their goals, and chosen three ways to achieve them, it is time to get ready to take action. The reason people don't already have what they want is because they don't know how to get it. In addition to the actual steps your students will take, they also have to **believe** they can achieve their goals, and **change** their self image and behavior while accepting the discomfort change may bring.

Monday—Image and Feel Success

People perform the way they see themselves. So one of the first steps toward goal achievement is to change a person's self image to include their goal. There are many ways to do this—one of which is to have your students "image" themselves as already having achieved their goal.

Ask your students to step into their future and imagine they already have their goal—they are doing it or they have it and are using it. What do they see? What do they hear? What do the feel? Smell? Taste? Where are they? Who is with them? Be sure they are "in" their picture, not just observing it. How do they feel having their goal fulfilled?

Tuesday—Affirmations For Success

Have your students again image their goal, with the feelings of fulfillment. Then have them create an affirmation (review affirmations from the first week) such as, "I keep my mind on my work until it is done," "I have an XQ2 model racing car," or "I have many friends." Have your students write their affirmation on a 3x5 card or a small piece of paper. Tell them to image their goal and repeat their affirmation when they get up in the morning and before they go to sleep at night—and as often as they want to during the day. Note: Some of your students may have already achieved their goal—just have them choose another one for these lessons.

If your students write a negative affirmation, such as "I won't eat candy," have them change it to a positive—"I eat only what's good for me!"

Wednesday—Act As If . . . To Achieve Success

Children are great actors. They often believe they themselves can't do something, yet when told to "act like" their friend Bob, who **can** do it, they perform beautifully! So when they are faced with a challenge, tell them to act as if, or perhaps pretend, they can do it.

Today, tell your students to image their goal, repeat their affirmation, and then pretend they are doing it. If possible, let them role play their goals.

Thursday—The Discomfort of Success

Some of your students may be feeling some anxiety from their changed behavior or self image. They are out of their comfort zone and may seek the comfort of old habits and self images—leading them into a vicious cycle.

F alse
E vidence
A ppearing as
R eal

Hooray! I'm changing!

The way to break out of this vicious cycle is to welcome the discomfort—greet it as an indication of change—"I'm on my way!"

Have your students draw the vicious cycle, giving it the most vicious face they can. Then have them draw how and where they will break the cycle by recognizing the discomfort as an indication of successful change!

Friday—Vary Behavior For Success

There is no such thing as a "free lunch." If your students are going to have what they want—to accomplish their goals—they will have to take action.

Holding their goal in their mind, and acting as if . . . , they can try those three ways to achieve their goal. And if they don't get it, they can try three more ways until the outside world matches the goal in their mind!

Children naturally do this—have you ever heard a child try 47 different ways to get something they want from their parents? Or watched a 10 year old with a Rubic cube or an electronic game? Help your students use this ability to vary their behavior by giving them various problems or brain teasers to solve and letting them get in groups and come up with solutions. Choose problems that are appropriate for their interest and age—use complex math "story" problems, interpersonal situations, mazes, puzzles, etc. Tell them to imagine the problem solved while they "pretend" they know how to do it. Then go to it! Praise them for their ability to try many ways. If they are stuck, tell them to act as if they could think of another way. Let frustration be a trigger to creativity.

If it's going to be, it's up to me!

Week of _____

MONDAY	Image and Feeling	Try it yourself! Image and feel your goal: My Goal:
	Time_____	
TUESDAY	Affirmation	An affirmation for my goal:
	Time_____	
WEDNESDAY	Act As If...	I will act as if I...
	Time_____	
THURSDAY	Break The Vicious Cycle	The discomfort of change means— I'm on my way!
	Time_____	
FRIDAY	Vary Behavior	3 more ways to achieve my goal
	Time_____	

WEEK 19

Testing For Success

Monday—Testing to Know: Did I Get It?

While taking action to achieve a goal, it is important to keep in mind your outcome, not only to focus your efforts, but to be able to recognize the achievement of your goal. How often have you had someone ask you to do something, you agreed, and then they continued to give you reasons why you should do it? They were so wrapped up in their plan to convince you that they didn't notice when they succeeded!

After doing something to achieve a goal, ask, "Did I get what I wanted?" Remember back to the goal and how you wanted to feel—what you wanted to see, hear, etc. Do you have it now? Does it match?

Teach your students this procedure. Use several examples of goals in interpersonal relationships, as well as with experiences and material objects. Then ask them to apply this matching procedure to their goal.

Tuesday—Test to Know When To Exit

After choosing a goal, doing something, and testing to see if you got it, it is very important to exit from the procedure. If you got what you wanted—great! Enjoy it and then move on to something else. If you didn't get it, it is important to know how long to keep trying to get it. If you have tried three ways, three more ways, and even three more ways, and still didn't get it—let it go. Find another goal that will satisfy your original intent. Some people make themselves miserable trying for an impossible goal. Choose a new goal.

Teach your students to exit after striving for something. Take them through several examples. In your teaching, help them to notice the endings of lessons, units, etc. Each ending is a new beginning!

Wednesday—Streamline And Test

Now it's time to put together and streamline the whole goal procedure: choosing and evaluating a **specific** goal, imagining and feeling the goal accomplished, stating an affirmation, acting as if . . . while varying their behavior; keeping the goal in mind for matching with the outcomes they are getting, recognizing their success, and/or choosing another goal.

Briefly review all steps from the past week by talking your students through the procedure for some specific goal. Choose another example and go through it again, combining steps, for example:

| specific goal | — | ways to get it | — | Act | — | Does it match? | — | Yes! Hooray! |
| | | | | | | | | No. Choose new goal. |

Take your students through this several times, or better yet, pair them up and have them talk each other through the steps for specific goals of their own.

In the future, notice how they use this strategy. Continue to use it with the children in a natural way, while planning an event, earning money for a field trip, etc.

Thursday—Testing Implications For Teaching

Before you begin to teach something, predict what your students will be able to do after learning. Have a specific, sensory based outcome in mind (they will be able to 1 . . . 2 . . . 3 . . .).

Sometimes it is appropriate to tell your students what you want them to learn before you teach and review what they have learned after the lesson.

Today, choose an appropriate lesson—

1. Establish your own sensory based outcome. My goal is:
2. Tell your students what they'll be expected to learn;
3. Review the important points:

Friday—Taking Tests

There are different kinds of testing that will give various qualities of information. The most simple is to directly ask for information or ask the students to perform a skill they have learned. This will let you know if they can perform in a testing situation.

To discover if they can use the skill or apply learnings in other situations, ask them to do an actual task or to use a skill in another situation.

When possible, it is best to observe how they use the learned skills and knowledge in their everyday life.

Notice how you test your students. Are you getting the quality of information you want?

Teach your students **how** to take a test.

- Relax
- Trust their intelligent guessing
- Do easy questions first and then go back to the harder ones
- Pace themselves to the allotted time
- Move on when they get stuck

Today, give them a test to practice on. Test them on something they are fairly familiar with so they can pay attention to learning **how** to take a test.

I test to find out if I've accomplished my goal.

Week of _____

MONDAY   Did I Get It?   Did I get it? Did my students learn
                                       the lesson?

                Time_____

TUESDAY   Exit!   Did they learn this lesson?
                                       No—plan for reteaching or review
                                       Yes—Great! What's next?

                Time_____

WEDNESDAY   Streamline   Go through this with a goal of your own:

                                                                      --Yes
                                       specific---ways to---Act---Does it
                                       goal   get it   match? --No

                Time_____

THURSDAY   Implications   Tell your students what you want
                                       them to learn!

                Time_____

FRIDAY   Tests   Observe: Did they use what I taught
                                       them while they took the test? _____
                                       _____
                                       _____
                                       _____
                                       _____

                Time_____

WEEK 20

Test Yourself—Semester Review, Evaluation And Goal Setting

Monday—Review Goals

Go over past lessons to choose this week's curriculum. Choose areas your students need further fun. As you review:

List your successes here:

_____

_____

_____

_____

List problem areas here:

_____

_____

_____

_____

Tuesday—Problems Are Opportunities: Goals

Review the problem areas, deciding which ones are the "Worry Can," which ones you want to exchange or reframe, and which ones you will seek a solution for. Keeping the feeling of your successes, choose goals to turn these opportunities into even more successes!

Goals:

Wednesday—Plan To Reach Your Goals

Make a definite plan for each goal and a master plan, including a timetable.

Yea!

Thursday—Future Thinking For Goals

Imagine how your class will be as you turn your goals into successes, one after another.

Friday—Goals: Do It!

Begin. Take some step—do one thing to start on your way.

Today I will:

_____

_____

_____

_____

_____

_____

Plans and dreams to create your perfect classroom.

Week of _____

MONDAY

Plan your week—Choose lessons to review

Time: _____

TUESDAY

Songs
Camera Game
Future Thinking
Brag Time
Success Book
Praise & Compliment
A+ Student
Treasure Map
Sanctuary
Guessing Game

Time: _____

WEDNESDAY

Grade own Papers
Attention Game
Directions Game
Color Game
Visual Imagery
Proofreading
Secretary Game
Memory Aids

Time: _____

THURSDAY

Tape Recorder Game
What It's Like To Be...
Awareness
Thankful Books
Choose Goals
Solution Screen
Problem Solving
Worry Can

Time: _____

FRIDAY

Testing
Perfect Anything
Write a Letter
Signal Words

Time: _____

I review my work and set new goals.

WEEK 21

Organization—Save Time And Effort

Each person perceives and organizes the world in his own unique way. The ability to organize the outer world, as well as mind processes, can be learned. Good organization reduces conflict, confusion, and wasted time.

Some people are great at organization. (V) They may see the whole picture, or they are able to mix ideas together and come up with new ones. (K) Or they may be easily able to sequentialize events through time (linear). Everyone has their own preferred way of organizing. Some methods are better for some types of organizational tasks than others.

We can teach organizational strategies and techniques to those who have no good methods and to those whose preferred organizational strategies don't work well for a particular task. You already do this by listing the daily schedule, diagramming sentences, using time lines, charts, graphs and diagrams, and teaching acronyms (i.e. EGBDF).

The better you organize what is taught, the better the learning will be.

For example, try memorizing this secret code for one minute:

1 = ⌟ 2 = ⊔ 3 = ∟ 4 = ⌝ 5 = ☐

6 = ⊏ 7 = ⌐ 8 = ⊓ 9 = ⌜

Time yourself for one minute. Then try writing it. How much quicker do you think it could be learned if it were taught with this pattern?

1	2	3
4	5	6
7	8	9

Monday—Organized Environment

Notice the organization of the classroom and the daily schedule. Is it providing an environment where the children will conclude that there is structure in the world and they will be able to understand it? Notice the things you want to change and how you will change them. Then begin to do it.

Tuesday—Organize Desks

Clean or messy desks, the style of work habits, the condition of handed in assignments, etc., may indicate whether or not a child believes he can cope with the situation he is in. Give the children time and incentive to keep their desks clean and neat. Have the condition of their work be as important as correct answers. Teach them to have materials ready and to schedule their time for finishing assignments.

Today: clean out and organize desks so materials will be ready. Tell your students how long they have to do this, and help them pace their activity by the clock to finish on time. Plan something enjoyable for them to do when they are finished.

Wednesday—Room Organization

Let the children participate in the structure and running of the room. Teach them procedures and let them have responsibilities in such areas as attendance, room maintenance, passing and checking papers, cleaning up, etc. Today, choose something you have not used student help for. Teach them what you want them to do, assign a task, and supervise them doing it.

Thursday—Making A Change For Organization

Discuss the benefits of organization. List the benefits, e.g., save time, learn with more understanding, able to find things or predict what will come next, etc. Tell the children to choose one thing they would like to organize. Give them time to do it now or make a plan of how they will do it. Let them work with a partner to get organizational ideas.

Friday—Teaching Organization

People will tell you how they are trying to organize and understand they'll say, "Show me how it goes;" "I can't grasp this;" or "Tell me how it is again." Use what you know about matching a person's preferred mode to help organize them. For example, drawing a diagram won't help someone who's trying to get in tune with something unless you talk them through it one idea at a time.

Be aware of your student's level of understanding in at least one of your lessons today. Draw diagrams, tell stories, or walk them through it. Do what is necessary to hear that sign of understanding from every student: "Oh—now I get it!" Then notice how **you** feel from succeeding at your job!

Here are a couple of organizational patterns for some of the material we have covered so far:

Time	Self (Teacher)	For and About the Other (Student)
From The Past	old beliefs view of the world	beliefs view of the world context of what they know now retrieve what is memorized review
In The Present	notice own thinking (visual, auditory or kinesthetic) choose my state of mind create new beliefs notice habits	notice eye cues notice signal words test for success try 3 ways and notice if achieved teach in all modes put in context
Into The Future	goal set problem solve change habits affirmations	future think bridge to other subjects schedule act as if . . . A+

Week of _____

MONDAY	Things I will organize and structure:	
	Time: _____	
TUESDAY	Clean Desks	Clean your desk too!
		Give yourself a pat on the back when you are done!
	Time: _____	
WEDNESDAY	Room Organization	Jobs students can help with:
	Time: _____	
THURSDAY	Make a Change	What I've learned from my students about organization:
	Time: _____	
FRIDAY	Teaching Applications	Concept:
		Applications:
	Time: _____	

I create an environment where
children find order.

WEEK 22

Discipline And Control—Use Your Power

The more choices you have for behavior, the more effective you'll be. In your teaching experience, you have developed many techniques that work. Here are some more.

Remembering that children want to learn and intend well, strive to change only what is necessary to direct their behavior in a positive, productive way. Use what they are already doing and make it work for them.

Monday—Match and Lead For Discipline

If your students are already involved in something when it's time for class to begin, you can win their attention without breaking their mood or coming across like the great dictator by simply matching them and leading them where you want them to go. This doesn't mean acting just like them or using their language, since it isn't necessary to match them completely. You can choose among many things to match: posture, quickness of movement, voice tone and level, intensity or level of feeling. Match them especially in those things you want them to continue during the lesson, i.e., aliveness, interest, their attention, passion, responsiveness. As you get control of their attention, smoothly lead them by slowing your movements and lowering your tone to the one you use for teaching. Watch them turn to their desks and books without feeling pushed.

Do this today!

Tuesday—Utilization For Discipline

If you have a problem situation, use it to advantage. The child who bullies or bosses can be in charge of library books, giving him a legitimate outlet for his desire for power. The P.A. interrupts a lecture—ask, "Any other comments?" and return to the lecture. A leaky roof can be an example of the force of gravity for the science lesson you are giving. These events are not "interruptions" in life—they **are** life. By your example, show that all of life is relevant and can teach us or show us something.

Today, use events. Watch for them. They'll be there!

Wednesday—Polarity Response In Discipline

Use the children's natural desire to their advantage. Some children have a polarity or opposite response as their natural response to almost everything. Use it. Just be sure you take the opposite of what you want them to do, think, or be and exaggerate it. Bob comes in complaining that the kids are teasing him and it isn't fair. Take his side and exaggerate. "Those kids ought to go to the principal, the police, jail—the electric chair even is too good for them!" And watch Bob flip to, "Well, that's ok, they are my friends, too." He knows he's been heard and understood. This isn't for everyone, but it works for some kids. Try it. Be sure you are on his side in your heart. Like any tool, this can be used for bad or good.

Thursday—Positive Intent in Discipline

When a child acts inappropriately, look for his positive intent and help him find a better way to achieve it, e.g., a child who teases may be looking for friends. Teach him some friend-making behavior. Tell him to try and come back and tell you what happened. A child who cheats wants a good grade. Tell him exactly what he has to do to earn the grade he wants and help him make a plan to achieve it.

Friday—Positive Commands In Discipline

You are giving embedded commands all the time, such as, "When you get your work done, here are some crossword puzzles." The embedded command is "get your work done." Become aware of the embedded commands in your conversation. Be sure you give the commands you want. Instead of, "I hope you **don't forget your homework**," say "I hope you **remember your homework.**" Instead of "**Don't fall,**" say, "**Be careful.**"

Today, as you notice the commands you give—make them positive.

Give yourself a pat on the back for trying new ideas!

Will you wash the 'bored'?

I lead children to positive behavior.

Week of _____

MONDAY	Match and Lead	How I used matching and leading:
TUESDAY	Utilization	Events and how I used them:
WEDNESDAY	Polarity Response	Results of using polarity response: (remember a loving heart)
THURSDAY	Positive Intent	Positive intent I discovered and aided:
FRIDAY	Positive Commands	Commands I used:

WEEK 23

Create Your Environment In Pictures And Words

We create our own environment and the circumstances of our life by how we think, and the actions we take as a result of our thinking. If we don't like what we have created, only we can change it.

Monday—Pictures In Your Environment

Notice the pictures and sayings you have hanging in your room. Are they positive, encouraging, life enhancing?—or diminishing, frightening? Look at each one and notice how you feel. What is the story of the picture? Is it something you want in your life? The pictures and sayings you have around you become blueprints of your life. If you don't like it—change it! Begin by changing those pictures.

Do this with your students. Teach them to notice pictures in the classroom so they can go home and do it in their own rooms. How many nightmares will go away when they remove the picture of the tiger? Today discuss all the pictures, posters, and sayings in your classroom. How do your students feel about them? Which ones do they want to keep and which ones do they want to remove?

Tuesday—Internal Pictures In Your Environment

A young girl moved with the ease of a tightrope walker across a board laid on the ground. Her father put it on supports two feet above the ground and she became clumsy and fell often. What pictures did she create in the environment of her mind to give her grace in one instance and clumsiness in the other? Even more than changing the pictures in your room, changing the pictures in your mind will have a dramatic effect on your life.

Notice your own thinking—have you ever imagined falling on the ice and then done it? Imagined dropping something just before it fell? If you don't like it—change it. Imagine moving with dexterity and ease and notice your gracefulness and skill.

Today, have the children do some motor activity (e.g., a dance movement, calisthenics, finger or hand movement, handwriting, etc.). Then discuss the effect of the pictures in their mind. Have them imagine doing the same activity with gracefulness and ease, performing it correctly and perfectly. Imagine each arm, leg, hand, and how it will move perfectly. Then have them do the activity again. Notice the changes. Encourage the children to use this in other areas of their lives.

Wednesday—Positive Phrases In Your Environment

What you say to the children will have a direct effect on their actions. The mother who says, "Don't fall," or "Watch out" will have an accident prone child. The mother who says "Be careful," or "Put it down gently," will have a careful, skillful child. Children live up to (or down to) the image we have of them.

Today, notice your phrasing as you give instructions. Say, "Remember to . . .", or "Walk quietly." Notice your negative phrases and write them here. Then create positive phrases to use in their place.

Change _____   to _____
Change _____   to _____
Change _____   to _____
Change _____   to _____

Thursday—Internal Phrases In Your Internal Environment

Words the children have heard all their lives have become the internal phrases they use in their daily lives. Children will tell you what some of their phrases are as they talk to themselves or others. Notice what they say about themselves if they've failed or made a mistake. Many children are eager to apply negative phrases to others who fail, such as "stupid!" or "Clumsy!" These are probably the same phrases they use on themselves or have heard from others. Teach children new positive phrases they can add to their already productive phrases or use to replace negative, self-defeating phrases. Talk about what phrases the girl in the example on Tuesday might have used as she walked the tightrope with ease, and as she became clumsy. List positive phrases children can use as they try new or difficult things. Have each child choose or create a positive phrase or an affirmation to make a poster of. Decorate your classroom delightfully with the positive posters!

Friday—Do it!

Teach the children to use these positive phrases, pictures, and feelings often throughout their day. Tell them to choose a phrase to use each morning as they wake and begin to picture the possibilities for their day. Encourage your students to build positive feelings as they image and affirm their abilities and worth.

Begin their school day by having them image all the successful work they will accomplish that day. Have them imagine how their papers will look done neatly and in their best handwriting. Have them write "I can do it" on challenging papers. Use these ideas in even more creative ways!

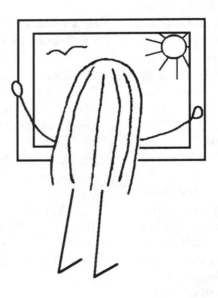

I create my environment!

Week of _____

MONDAY	Change Pictures In the Room:	Pictures I'll change:
	Time: _____	
TUESDAY	Internal Pictures	Image teaching successfully, competently handling all situations with elegance and grace
	Time: _____	
WEDNESDAY	Positive Phrases	Positive phrases I use with my students:
	Time: _____	
THURSDAY	Internal Phrases	Positive phrases I use with myself:
	Time: _____	
FRIDAY	Do it!	I will:
	All day	

Yea!

WEEK 24

Create Your Environment In Feelings

The positive images and phrases you create will become the blueprint for your life only if you have the corresponding feeling. Some cultures teach children to change their feelings as easily and readily as changing internal phrases and pictures.

Monday—Change Feelings

Tell the children to picture a favorite place, then change their picture. Have them listen internally to a favorite song, then change it to another one. Tell them they can change their feelings as easily as they can change pictures and sounds. Tell them to feel angry . . . happy . . . confused . . . sad . . . joyful . . . surprised . . . delighted . . . etc. Just as they readily changed their feelings in this exercise, they can change their feelings when they are in a situation where they don't like how they feel. Until now, this skill was not generally taught in our culture, as it is in some other cultures. Anything that another person can do is possible for us to do also. Have your students imagine a situation where they don't like their feelings— change their feelings while imagining the same situation in pictures and sounds. Tell them to let you know when this works for them in their lives.

Tuesday—Position Of Competence—Feelings

Relax and experiment: Remember a time when you were successful and confident. Notice your body position and breathing right now. Your body is responding and assuming your position of competence. This body position and breathing can be yours whenever you want. Remember a time you wished that you could have handled something differently? Notice your feelings— want to feel competent again? Assume your posi-

tion of competence and the corresponding breathing. Feel it! Breathe it! This is yours to have whenever you want. You need never feel weak again. Just assume the position and **breathe.**

Give this experience to your students. Recreate the experiment for them.

Also, be sure your students are in a position of competence before asking them to perform anything so they can achieve their highest. Tell them to sit up . . . breathe . . . think thoughts of success . . . and begin.

Wednesday—Synesthesia—Create Feelings

Did you ever "feel" the music? Or notice your mood change when seeing a picture? Sometimes our feelings are influenced by internal pictures and sounds of which we are unaware. We are "feeling" an image or words instead of seeing an image or hearing words.

Sometimes when you are feeling a way you don't want to feel, become aware of your internal images, sounds or dialogue. **See** the images, hear the words and sounds. Then change them by creating those images, sounds or words that will cause you to feel the way you want to feel!

Today, play with synesthesia with your students. Play music for them to "feel." Tell them to "see" colors come out of people's mouths instead of words. Show pictures for them to "hear." Then introduce them to the idea of getting feelings from unconscious pictures, sounds and words, and also the method of changing it.

Thursday—Positive Word In A Moment Of Anger—Feelings

Teach your students to use the emotional energy of their anger to change their lives. Tell them to repeat "love," "peace," or some other positive word when they feel angry. The emotional energy will attach to the word and bring them love and peace, bringing with it the opportunity for a new perspective and understanding. Try it yourself and give it to your students.

Friday—Carbon Copy—Feelings

You keep the original and give away the carbon copy of any words or thoughts toward people. This is how our minds work. What do you want in your life? Health—love—peace—competence—excellence. Think of this for others—wish it for them—and get it for yourself!

Today, give your students small pieces of carbon paper. Tell them that our minds keep the original of whatever we give away. Let them write messages (or draw pictures) for others—but they must keep the original! After they have done this for a time, have them look at their originals. This is what they are building their life of. If they don't like it, change it! Let them write new messages of thought for other people.

Optional: Lead them in a meditation of positive, joyous, successful thoughts for their family, friends and all others in the world.

I create my feelings!

Week of _____

MONDAY	Change Feelings	Experiment with your own feelings now and in the future—changing them at will
	Time: _____	
TUESDAY	Position of Competence	A time I felt particularly competent
	Time: _____	
WEDNESDAY	Synesthesia	Experiment with your next headache or tension. Notice your visual images—change them. Notice your auditory messages or sounds—change them. Feel better!
	Time: _____	
THURSDAY	Positive Word In a Moment of Anger	The positive word I'll use the next time I feel angry is: _____
	Time: _____	
FRIDAY	Carbon Copy	Messages I give to others:
	Time: _____	

WEEK 25

Winning Relationships With Others

To a degree, we can create our own environment of people around us and influence how those people treat us.

Monday—Compliments In Relationships

Discuss with your students how they feel when they receive compliments, what kind of compliments they prefer, and what kind of compliments bother them. Practice in a role play situation, giving and receiving compliments.

Their assignment is to give three compliments today. Tell them to notice the response of the person they give to. Discuss things to look for in evaluating the response. Have them change their way of giving compliments if the person seems uncomfortable.

Tuesday—Be An Action Person In Relationships

Discuss their experience yesterday in giving compliments.

Today, discuss being an action person. There are people who act and people who wait for others to act before they react. Discuss what actions people do (say hello first, ask others to play, etc.). If other people can be action people, then they can learn to be so also. Have them choose one hour each day to act like an action person.

Wednesday—Anchoring In Relationships

Discuss experiences of giving compliments and acting like action people.

Anchors are triggers that bring a specific response each time. Remember the aroma of freshly baked cookies?—The smile on the face of someone you love?—Your favorite song?—The touch of a friend? Notice your response. These anchors will consistently bring the same response.

The way you touch, praise, and smile at your students will establish anchors you can use again to bring back their feeling of success. Today, begin establishing those anchors with your students. Get to know them individually—what makes them feel happy and successful. And when they're feeling happy or successful, give them a smile, a touch, or a word of praise that you can use again to bring back that feeling.

Thursday—Getting The Response You Want From Others In Relationships

Discuss with your students that they already know how to get others mad or upset—teasing a younger brother, sassing Mom or Dad, "forgetting" to do something Mom asked. How powerful they are! They can use this same power to get people to feel good, to be happy around them, or to do something for them. They can get people to treat them the way they want to be treated.

Have them choose some response they want from someone and think of three ways they can get it. Tell them to try it for homework and you'll discuss it tomorrow.

Friday—Relationships Review

Discuss their success at getting the responses they wanted. If they got it—great! If they didn't get the response they wanted, have them decide if they still want to get the same response or if they want to go for something else. If they still want to—have them choose three new ways to get it.

Review giving and receiving compliments and being an action person. Tell them they can keep on doing these things next week, next year, and so on. Have them image times in the future they will be using these ideas.

I am responsible for the response I get from others.

Week of _____

MONDAY	Compliments	Three compliments I gave today: 1. 2. 3.
	Time: _____	
TUESDAY	Be An Action Person	This is when I will act like an action person:
	Time: _____	
WEDNESDAY	Anchoring	SMILE TOUCH PRAISE
	Time: _____	
THURSDAY	Get The Response You Want From Others	Person: The response I want: 3 ways I will try: 1. 2. 3. Evaluate success:
	Time: _____	
FRIDAY	Discussion And Review	3 more ways or something else I want:
	Time: _____	

I create winning relationships with others.

WEEK 26

Communication With Others

We communicate in many ways; through our actions, gestures, touches, sounds—and through our use of language. We may or may not have a shared meaning for particular words, phrases, gestures, etc. For us to think we "understand" someone else or they "understand" us is no more realistic than thinking all people are alike! Yet both the "talker" and the "listener" can do much to insure good communication.

Monday—How Do I Tell It?—Communication

The talker must realize that the listener does not yet know—and will only know—what he, the talker, communicates.

A talker naturally communicates differently to different people or groups of people. Discuss this with your students and give examples or role play these things to be considered.

1. Age—How do you talk to a grown up, your peers, a younger person, a baby, a pet?

2. Knowledge of subject—You have a lot more explaining to do when talking about a home run to someone who's never heard of baseball. On the other hand, you and a friend can share a glance that says, "Joe is behaving in the same old way again."

3. Predicates—From listening to a person's speech, you can learn if they "see" how things are, "hear" what you say, or "feel" their way through. Then you can "show" them, "tell" them, or give them a "grasp" on the subject by using the same type of predicates they use ("let me draw you a picture of this," "in other words," or "in smoother terms,").

4. When you're trying to persuade someone to do something, you use your knowledge of them—their interests, needs, weak spots and strategies.

   a. Who gives in when you whine . . . yell . . . pout . . . or are super nice?

   b. Who would give you what you want for a hug, a piece of candy, money?

   c. If Bobby always says, "Come on, it'll be lots of fun!" use similar words in persuading him, and watch how fast he comes! As an optional exercise: Group your students in threes. Part 1—A tries to convince B to do something. (Then B to C, and C to A)—Notice each person's strategy. Part 2—Do the same thing again, only this time use a person's strategy on himself! Discuss the outcome.

You have only learned to do these things because they work. Your study of what you do, and how you can do it, can aid you in consciously using these principles to further communication and "understanding."

Tuesday—The Listener—Getting The Story In Communication

It is the listener's job to make sure he hears and understands what is being said. Teach these three principles to your students:

The listener can ask the talker to:

1. Repeat information—"I didn't hear what you said; will you please repeat that?"

2. Be specific—"Who do you mean by 'he?' When? How did he do it?" etc.

3. Say it in other words—"Tell me again in another way, please."

Give your students an opportunity to practice by telling them a story and purposely leaving out words, ideas, etc., or pair them up and let them listen to and question each other.

Tell your students you want them to begin asking you these questions as you teach. Praise them for putting this lesson to use in their daily lives.

Wednesday—The Listener—Congruence In Communication

The listener can learn much from how a person talks (voice tone, inflection, choice of language in terms of dialect, slang, etc.) as well as from nonverbal language (body posture, distance from and position to listener, facial expression, etc.). We respond to these cues whether we are aware of them or not. Have you ever found yourself backing away from someone without realizing he had encroached on "your space"?

Today, teach your children to pay attention to voice tone/inflection and nonverbal language while they listen to someone talk. Teach them also to compare this message with the verbal message. Are the two congruent? Do they match? If not, which do they believe?

Exercise 1: Experiment with voice tone and inflection. Say a sample sentence or phrase using different inflection and voice tone, e.g., "Come here," "Did you see what she did?" Encourage your students to think of sentences that can be taken many ways, and then give them a chance to express many meanings for one sentence by varying their voice tone, tempo, and inflection. If

your students are sufficiently mature, explain and experiment with sarcasm.

Exercise 2: Have a student nonverbally "act out" an attitude, such as impatience, delight, surprise, anger, etc., while the other students observe and guess the attitude.

Exercise 2a: Have two sets of cards—one with attitudes, one with feeling phrases such as "I like that!", "I'm angry," "I'm happy," etc. A student chooses one attitude card and one phrase card and does them simultaneously. The two may or may not match. Let the rest of the class decide what the nonverbal message is and whether or not they are congruent. Which do they believe? Why?

Thursday—Outcome In Communication

After comprehending the message, the listener may want to respond. He then becomes the talker. He should decide not only what he wants to say, and how to say it, but also what outcome he hopes to achieve (effect a compromise, get him to consider options, add information, etc.).

Teach your students the strategy of:

1. Keeping your specific outcome in mind, while keeping:
2. a positive feeling as though it is already achieved;
3. Vary your words, behavior, etc.
4. Notice the response of the other person until:
5. your desired outcome matches what is happening **OR** you decide to quit and do something else.

The meaning of your message is the response it gets. If you don't like the response—change your message!

Exercise: Group your students in threes—A, a talker, B, a listener, and C, an observer. The talker decides on a specific outcome (get the listener to agree to go somewhere, understand and repeat a concept, tell what he knows about something, etc.). The listener listens and responds. The observer watches and keeps the others on track.

The talker keeps his outcome in mind and continually matches it with what's really happening—STOPPING when his outcome is achieved **OR** he decides he won't be able to achieve it.

Give students a chance to participate in all three positions.

Discuss and answer any questions.

Friday —Communication Strategy

Put it all together. Review how the talker develops an **outcome** and decides **how** to get it. He then begins and keeps his outcome in mind while noticing the response he gets, varying his communication until he gets the **response** he wants. During this time, the listener is giving **feedback** to let the talker know if he understands or needs more information and notices the voice tone/inflection and nonverbal behavior, checking if the message is **congruent** or mixed. The listener also does his own **thinking**, forms his own **conclusions** and **outcome,** and then becomes a talker. It's now the other's turn to act as listener. This process goes back and forth, much as tennis players serve, receive, and return the ball.

Exercise: "On the Ball"

Group your students in threes—an observer and two who communicate. One has a ball with "talker" on it, the other has a ball with "listener" on it. The observer acts as umpire to make sure they follow the rules. If a person has the listening ball, he can only ask questions to clarify and indicate whether or not he understands. If he wants to tell the other person something, he must ask for the talking ball. The talker can give him the ball or keep it until he has finished his message and/or achieved his outcome and is ready to listen. Then they exchange balls. They keep switching balls as their positions change. Give them topics to begin with (should we change recess, parents are too strict, etc.) or let them go with their own ideas. Give each child a chance to be a player and an umpire. Be sure to use these good communication techniques with your students. They'll be noticing!

The response I get is the meaning of my messaage.

Week of _____

MONDAY	How do I tell it?	Notice today how you package information differently for different people.
	Time: _____	
TUESDAY	The Listener—Getting The Story	Really listen to someone—let them know what you do and don't understand—ask for more information. **Get** their message!
	Time: _____	
WEDNESDAY	Congruence	As you listen to someone, notice if their tone/inflection and body language match their verbal message. If not, which do you believe?
	Time: _____	
THURSDAY	Outcome	Decide on an outcome—change your behavior and notice the response. Did you get it?
	Time: _____	
FRIDAY	On the ball	As you talk to people today, imagine a "talker" or "listener" ball in your hands—notice as you pass the balls back and forth.
	Time: _____	

WEEK 27

Use Of Language To Enrich Our Experience Of The World

We experience the world through our senses. We see, hear, feel, taste, and smell. As children, when we learned language, we gave words to our experience. Thus, a certain set of feelings, images, touches, tastes and smells (a certain experience) became associated with a particular word. That word became an anchor or association for that experience. As the years pass, we may have begun to rely on the words themselves and become less aware of our actual experience—the taste, sight, feel, smell, and sound of life—and in effect, become strangers to ourselves. But the use of language is a habit. We can develop language habits that bring us closer to our experience once again.

Monday—Language—Pronouns

When the first person used "they"—he probably knew what people he meant. Through time, the use of "they" has come to mean some nameless authority that many of us blindly obey. "They say— ". Well, who is they?

Asking "Who specifically is they?" can be a first step toward freeing us from the tyranny of a limiting language habit. Today, when you hear your students using "they," or any other pronoun in an unspecified way, ask them "Who specifically?" or "What specifically?" When a child says, "I really like it!", your question, "What exactly do you like?" will direct the child back to his experience. Then his description of what he likes will come closer to his actual experience. He will enrich his experience and you will understand him better.

Tuesday—Language—Adjectives

Getting in the habit of using adjectives and descriptions not only enriches another's understanding of our world, but also encourages us to more closely notice the world. Snow is just snow until we ski—then there is powder, corn snow, base, etc.

Today, have a lesson in noticing. Assemble objects for your students to touch, taste, smell, etc. —perhaps a strawberry and a crunchy cracker. Spend some time observing and noticing. List descriptive words. Then construct sentences about the object using these descriptive words. In the future, continue to encourage your students to provide full descriptions in their oral and written language.

Wednesday—Language—Adjectives That Compare

We naturally make comparisons to distinguish between objects, skills, experiences, etc. Words like more and less, and words with the suffixes -er and -est are tools that allow us to label these comparisons. Labels help us remember and allow us to communicate with others. When making comparisons, it is important to remember what is the basis for comparison and what objects, etc., are being considered in the comparison.

Today, with your class, look for differences among similar objects. Chart the comparisons in this manner to teach your students to form sentences that completely express the comparison:

Object, person experience being compared	Comparison more or less -er -est	Group being compared	Basis of comparison stated or implied
This Winter	is colder	than last Winter	according to the Weather service.
The blue chair	is the biggest	of our classroom	according to height.
This wool jacket	is more practical	than the cotton jacket	for keeping warm
Bob	is cuter	than Tom	according to Sue.

Then have your students, on their own, observe, form comparisons, and create sentences (written or oral).

When you notice comparative statements in your student's conversation, ask questions to draw out the complete comparisons: "Of what group?" "On what basis?" etc. This will increase conscious awareness of their experience.

Thursday—Language—Verbs Objects

Verbs describe an action. There is a subject (stated or implied) and sometimes an object. The more fully we specify the subject and the object, the closer our language is to representing our experience. For example, "The boys are chasing us," can be more specifically stated, "Bob and Joe are chasing May and me." "Bob is angry" creates a different impression than "Bob is angry at his brother."

Today as you notice your students' oral and written language, ask them to specify the subject and object of the verbs they use. Ask "Who did it?", "Happy about what?" etc.

Friday—Language—Adverbs and Prepositional Phrases

Encourage your students to more fully describe their experience. Today, use a chart like the one below to enrich sentences.

Encourage your students to fully express themselves with adverbs and adverbial phrases by asking, "How?" both in their written work and oral language.

Subject	Adverb	Verb	Object	How
Mary	gracefully	danced		on her toes
Joey	carefully	fixed	the toy	with his hammer
The door	quickly	closed		with a bang

Week of _____

MONDAY	Specify Pronouns	Who is THEY?
	Time: _____	
TUESDAY	Adjectives That Describe	Follow up with:
	Time: _____	
WEDNESDAY	Adjectives That Compare	Enrich your world— Be specific in your own comparisons!
	Time: _____	
THURSDAY	Verbs (Subject And Object)	When asking children questions about their experiences, be sure to tactfully and gently question them. Convey your interest and desire to know more about them and their experiences.
	Time: _____	
FRIDAY	Adverbs And Prepositional Phrases All day	

I encourage my students to more fully express themselves.

WEEK 28

Generalization—How We Create Our Beliefs

Three of the mind processes that let us learn, grow, survive, understand, and experience the world are Generalization, Deletion, and Distortion. Through these, we create a mind map of reality. But if we mistake our "map" for reality, these same processes limit us and keep us from learning, growing, and experiencing. Then we must challenge our beliefs to overcome obstacles and reconnect to reality.

Monday—Useful Generalizations

Generalizing is finding a pattern and believing it will hold true for all cases. It helps us learn and know what to expect.

Reggie was told by his Mom not to hit Sally, but she didn't say anything about not kicking her! He didn't generalize his mother's comment to not hurting another person. We learn by generalization. That's how we come to know that all those things with a back, seat, and four legs are to sit on. Watch a first grader laboriously count out: six blocks + one block = 7 blocks, 7 blocks + one block = 8 blocks, until they generalize and say, "Hey! a number plus one is just the next number!" Teach children to generalize what they've learned. You may have to point out examples that lead to a generalization. Then test the generalization to discover if you can find examples that contradict it.

Today, pick one subject and be explicit with your students about the generalizations involved. Teach them the concept of generalizing often in the days and weeks to come.

Tuesday—Limiting Generalizations

Overgeneralizing, or bringing a generalization to an inappropriate context, can be limiting.

Children may express situations that distress them in general terms. Careful questioning can reveal the actual incident that is causing them distress. For example:

Child: Amy hates me! (Generalization)
Ask: How do you know?
Child: Because she's angry.
Ask: What is she angry at?
Child: Her dad grounded her. (Specific)

Child: Kids don't get to have any fun!
        (Generalization)
Ask: Which kids?
Child: Me. I don't get to.
Ask: What can't you do?
Child: I can't play after school.
Ask: What stops you?
Child: I have to take the garbage out
first. (Specific)

As the child's language becomes more specific, his perception of the event changes, as in, "Is the glass half empty or half full?"

Begin today to notice situations like these. Question your students to release them from limiting generalization and bring them closer to their actual experience.

Wednesday—Exaggerate To Break A Generalization

Notice cue words such as all, each, every, any, none, no one, nothing, never, etc. These words signal possible limiting generalizations. If a child says, "Nobody ever pays attention to me," you can exaggerate the generalization: "You mean **nobody ever** pays **any** attention to you?" Exaggerate it to the point where it is obviously an untrue generalization. If a child says, "Everyone else can go," you can say, "The whole world will be there and you'll be the only person left!"

Begin today to expose limiting generalizations of that type.

Thursday—Contradictions To A Generalization

When someone presents a limiting generalization, ask them to search their memory for experiences that would contradict their generalization. Enough experiences will help them form a new generalization that successfully challenges the old one.

If they do not have a contradictory experience of their own, ask if they can imagine having such an experience or imagine someone else having it. The mind does not always know the difference between a real experience and a fully felt imagined experience.

Sometimes simply commenting on contradictions that are happening at the moment will challenge a limiting generalization. "I'm paying attention to you right now" is a response to someone who says nobody pays attention to them.

Friday—Breaking Related Generalizations

Sometimes children (and adults too) will form a generalization about two events that in reality are unrelated, e.g., "My mother is angry. My mother hates me." Break this generalization by first asking if they believe it is true. "Do you mean that if your mother is angry, she hates you?" If they affirm it, then switch persons and ask, "Does your being angry mean you hate your mother?" If they persist, continue to question—"Everytime? Has there ever been a time you were angry and didn't hate her? Can you imagine a time? Are you angry now? Do you hate her?" As you can see, the questions can go on and on, bringing the child closer to his experience.

As beliefs and generalizations change, people can learn and grow. Without the ability to change, we become stagnant.

Note: The models and generalizations in this book are only useful when we see them as maps. If we mistake them for reality, we limit ourselves. As you are using these models, be aware of the exceptions and the situations where they don't work or don't hold true. Create new hypotheses, new models—work with these and challenge them also. Keep growing!

I free myself of limiting generalizations!

Week of _____

MONDAY	Useful Generalization	Subject area: Generalize:
	Time: _____	
TUESDAY	Be Specific	Write the results of one successful challenge here
	Time: _____	
WEDNESDAY	Exaggerate	Be sensitive to the child's feelings. Laugh with him, not at him!
	Time: _____	
THURSDAY	Contradictions	A successful challenge!
	Time: _____	
FRIDAY	Complex Equivalence	A complex equivalent I discovered and challenged:
	All day	

WEEK 29

Deletion—Choosing What We Pay Attention To

We decide what we pay attention to and what we leave out. This is useful in focusing attention so we won't be overwhelmed by experience. It is limiting if we leave out parts of our experience that we need for a useful and complete model of our world (if we continually shut out one sense, shut out pertinent facts, or shut out our own part in a situation).

Monday—Useful Deletion

Help the children learn to focus in spite of distractions. Some children will be bothered by distractions in one sensory area more than others. Through discussion, help them to individually determine the distractions that are most bothersome to them and that they feel most helpless to correct. Then help them come up with creative ways they can use their strengths and abilities to prevent the distraction. Examples: Creating an imaginary force shield that keeps out distractions, making imaginary picture frames that help them focus on a page of reading, imaginary superheroes that blast unwanted sounds to smithereens before they can reach their ears. Help them with concrete ways to change their environment (move to the front of the room or find a quiet place to study).

Tuesday—Deletion of Nouns

As they speak, notice if the children have enough nouns for their verbs. Does each verb tell who, to whom, about what, etc. Notice if your students use proper endings on verbs. If they delete some of this material, ask: "Who did it?", "To whom?", "About what?", etc. Often simply recovering a full language expression of an event will enrich the sense and meaning of the experience.

Wednesday—Deletion of "Or"

Often people will remember they "must" or "should" do something, but they no longer know why or what will happen if they don't! Every "must" or "should" started out with an "or."

You must _____ or _____.
You should _____ or _____.

Through the years, the "or"s have been lost. Many "musts", "shoulds", and "shouldn'ts" are based on good reason. We want to keep those. But some "musts", "shoulds", and "shouldn'ts" are based on consequences that are no longer valid. These must be re-examined or we will be bound and limited by them. Ask "Or what will happen?" Often realizing the obsolete reason for doing something will release someone from a limiting behavior. Examining a consequence of a "must" or "should" will lead us to realize that it wouldn't be so awful after all—and allow us to experiment with a new behavior.

Notice the "musts", "shoulds", and "shouldn'ts" your students use. If you see them as limiting, ask for the "or" and give your students a chance to redecide.

Thursday—Deletion with "Can't"

Some people who say they can't do something, or that something is impossible, often have no idea of what stops them or makes it impossible. Ask "What prevents you?" or "What makes it impossible?" Finding out the actual hurdles aren't so insurmountable may permit people to escape from the limitation of "can't".

Notice how your students use "can't". Challenge the "can't" and offer them the possibility to succeed.

Friday—Deletion in Comparison

Children often make comparisons without fully considering what they are comparing. Today, perhaps in your English lesson, review comparison words and phrases. Talk about what is the basis for comparison. Help them discover what indeed they are comparing. This will help to make comparisons useful instead of limiting and ego destructing. In the future, in their daily conversation, watch for comparison words, and if the basis for comparison is deleted, ask questions to draw it out ("Prettier than who?", "Best in respect to what or who?", "Better at what?" etc.).

I choose what I will pay attention to!

Week of _____

MONDAY	Useful deletion	Distractions **I** want to screen:
	Time: _____	
TUESDAY	Be Specific	How I will do this:
	Time: _____	
WEDNESDAY	Must, Should	Shoulds I will demolish:
	Time: _____	
THURSDAY	Can't	Can'ts **I** will abolish:
	Time: _____	
FRIDAY	Comparisons	My limiting comparisons:
	Time: _____	

WEEK 30

Distortion—Altering Reality

Distorting the information that our senses bring in can be useful in many ways—planning our future, dreaming, creating artistically, exploring scientifically, and writing creatively, among other things. Distortion is limiting when people interpret events in such a way that they have no options for action or interpretation, such as a person who distorts all mistakes as "I'm stupid. I never should have tried anyway." The result is that any value in the mistake is lost, as well as the opportunity for growth and change. This week we will challenge some limiting distortions.

Monday—Distortion—Cause—Effect

Children often think that their feelings are entirely caused by the actions of others and that they have no control over their own thinking or feeling. Today, begin to challenge this type of erroneous thinking by asking them how specifically the others caused them to feel that way. Or say, "Do you mean that if (that person) didn't . . . then you wouldn't feel . . . ?" or "Every time someone . . . , do you have to . . . ?" Help them to recover the choices and options they have lost by their distorted thinking.

Tuesday—Mind Reading

Since adults so often successfully guess what is going on in the minds of children, children often come to believe that others can read their minds. Then they begin to think they can also read the minds of others, not realizing they are probably imagining how they themselves would think and feel in such a situation. Basing conclusions on "mind reading" instead of actual communication is another example of distorted thinking.

Today, challenge "mind reading" by asking "How do you know what he is asking?" or "How can you be sure I know what you are thinking?" Encourage your students to check out their "guesses" with the person involved. Make it into a life enhancing game.

Wednesday—"But"

Use of the word "but" sometimes implies that something is made impossible or necessary. This can be limiting when people unrealistically think that outside forces either prevent them or force them into doing something

"I want to do my homework, but . . ."
"I didn't mean to break that, but . . ."

Challenge by asking, "If . . . didn't happen, then you would do your homework?" or "What forces you to . . . ?"

When children realize that no one is preventing them or forcing them to do something, they can take responsibility for their own choices and decisions. Then **they** have the power to keep or change their decisions and choices. Continue to challenge "but" when it is limiting your students' choices or senses of self direction.

Thursday—Recognizing Nominalizations

Nominalizations are a form of distortion where processes are thought of as nouns (love is really not a noun, but a process—loving). Love isn't something we "get"—it's something we do! Yet people will say, "I need more love in my life." How much? A half a cup? Two gallons? Or they will say, "I can't think with all this confusion," or "I need help"—or more appreciation, happiness, attention, pleasure, etc.—or "I have too much loneliness, grief, guilt", etc.

Today, learn to recognize nominalizations. They act like nouns in a sentence, yet they are not a thing you can hear, see, touch, etc. Have your students search their reading books and minds for nouns and nominalizations. Give them the truck test. If you can imagine it in a truck, it's a noun—e.g., ball, car, Mom, etc. If you can't, it's a nominalization, e.g., decision, truth, balance, interest, accident, etc. With your class make a list of nouns and nominalizations.

Nouns	Nominalizations
plant	creation
table	importance

Friday—Challenging Nominalizations

When we turn processes into nouns, they become things that we may not have much control over.

However, when we change them back into verbs, they are something we can do. We can love, we can decide, value, etc. And then we regain control.

Today, demonstrate to you students how nominalizations are verbs masquerading as nouns. Ask them if they want "love," "happiness," "appreciation," etc. Tell them to hold out their hands and you'll give them some. Point out that these are **not** commodities that one person can give another. They are action verbs that a person must do!

Today, and in the future, notice nominalizations in your students' language. Challenge if they are limiting. Change them back into verbs. If someone says, "All this indecision is awful," ask "What is it that you haven't decided?" or if they say, "I need help," ask, "What do you want me to help you with?" Watch them regain control over their own lives.

I challenge limiting distortions!

Week of _____

MONDAY   Cause—Effect   People today think we live from the
                                      outside in—that external happenings
                                      create our feelings. It's just the opposite—
                                      we live from the inside out!

                Time: _____

TUESDAY   Mind Reading   Have your students play a game of guessing
                                      what the other person is thinking and then
                                      finding out if they are right. Hopefully
                                      they will notice they are wrong most of the
                                      time.

                Time: _____

WEDNESDAY   But   "But's" I will get rid of:

                Time: _____

THURSDAY   Recognizing   Some Nominalizations I use:

                Time: _____

FRIDAY   Challenging   Change them to:
                Nominalizations

                Time: _____

WEEK 31

Presuppositions—Using Your Power For Success

Presuppositions, another form of distortion, are word phrases that assume the truth of something in order for the rest of the situation or statement to make sense. "If Johnny becomes an A+ student, I'll be surprised." Because of the powerful nature of presuppositions, they must be used with care.

Presuppositions can be a most helpful tool in raising someone's confidence, expanding limits, or creating choice. If you say, "The beautiful way you read that poem brought tears to my eyes," the child may accept without question that he read beautifully. "Some of the other possibilities are—" presupposes that there are other choices. Our language is naturally full of presuppositions. Our goal is not to delete them, but to recognize them and be responsible for our use of them.

Some Common Presuppositions

1. Names, pronouns, descriptions

   The boy with the baseball bat came.
   (implies a boy had a baseball bat)

   Bob won.
   (implies someone named Bob)

   I gave it to her.
   (implies some female)

2. Who

   I gave the prize to the boy who won.
   (implies someone won)

   Who threw the airplane?
   (implies someone threw an airplane)

3. Time word phrases—when, before, after, during, as, etc.

   She told me when I was eating lunch.
   (implies I was eating lunch)

4. Number words

   Bob was fourth in line.
   (implies three people ahead of him)

5. Comparisons—er, more, best, less, etc.

   Joe was the best catcher.
   (implies there were other catchers)

6. Verbs that imply change—enter, leave, come, go, begin, start, stop, change, become, turn into, continue, etc.

   George stopped running and looked.
   (implies George had been running)

7. Adjectives and adverbs—lucky, strange, amazing, odd, know, realize, etc.

   I realize how nice Bob is.
   (implies Bob is nice)

8. If

   If you had asked me first, I would have said yes.
   (implies you didn't ask first)

9. Negative questions

   Didn't you finish it?
   (implies I thought you had finished it)

Monday—Recognize Presuppositions

Give examples for the students to notice what was presupposed. Have them look in their reading books or other books for more. Discuss some presuppositions in advertising ("We're #2. We try harder." "You deserve a break today.") Also discuss the presupposition implied in the situations of some ads (no friends until you use a mouthwash, etc.). Tell your students to listen to TV and radio ads and write them down to bring in to discuss. Ask them to also bring in newspaper and magazine ads.

Tuesday—Presuppositions In Advertising

Examine the presuppositions in the ads the children brought in. Find the assumptions and discuss whether they are necessarily true.

Wednesday—Student's Presuppositions

Learn to recognize the presuppositions in your students' language. It will give you insight into their model of the world and what they assume to be true. If you discover a limiting belief, bring it to the attention of the student. This will give him the chance to decide if he wants to hold or challenge his belief.

Thursday—Presupposition Praise

One of the most powerful ways to praise is indirectly, through the use of presuppositions. Telling a child, "Your hard work really improved your grade," or "I'm impressed with the ingenious way you figured that out" may cause a child to believe he is hard working or ingenious—and believing it, he will act like it!

Today, experiment with presuppositions as you praise your students. Use this power to create excellence!

Friday—Presuppositions In Implied Commands

Give implied commands to your students. They may do what you say without question if you presuppose the behavior you want. "When you complete your paper, put it on my desk," presupposes that they will finish the paper. Asking "Do you want to do it before or after recess?" implies they will do it.

Experiment with implied commands today. Notice the ones you already use, and use new ones to help you achieve your goals for your students.

I'm amazed at how quickly you did that!

I recognize presuppositions and use them carefully.

Week of _____

MONDAY	Recognize Presuppositions	Sources I'll use for this lesson:
	Time: _____	
TUESDAY	Presuppositions In Advertising	Ads to discuss
	Time: _____	
WEDNESDAY	Student's Presuppositions	Presuppositions I noticed in student language
	Time: _____	
THURSDAY	Presupposition POWER	Praise phrases:
	Time: _____	
FRIDAY	Implied Commands	Implied commands I successfully used:
	Time: _____	

WEEK 32

Anchoring—A Tool For Growth

Throughout the year, we have done anchoring in many ways. In the Attention Game, you were anchoring the students to your words, voice tone, and posture so they would become attentive when they perceived the "anchor." Your words of praise, your smile, and touch are all anchors, as is that certain tone of voice you use to let your students know you mean it and they'd better behave. Any stimulus that gives a consistent response is an anchor. Remember the smell of your Mom's chocolate chip cookies? That smell is an anchor that can take you back to childhood memories. Anchors can be a touch, word, image, etc.

Monday—Gathering Resources And Anchoring Them

Children often have skills and abilities they may have used once, may use outside of school, or may only have dreamed of doing. You can help them make full use of these abilities in a school setting by anchoring these abilities to their tasks. Decorate the room with their successfully completed papers and success slogans to anchor your students to their feeling of competence and success. Before starting a task, ask your students to remember past successes, or image their sanctuary with all its resources.

Tuesday—The Anchor Of One Time Learning

Anchors can occur in a very powerful way from one time learning. A young child proudly showed his just completed picture to Aunt Mary. Aunt Mary frowned and said, "Oh no! That's not how it's done—let me show you." The child felt terrible and concluded that it was bad to do some-thing the wrong way and to make a mistake. To this day, he feels terrible when he gets even one thing wrong, and he doesn't remember why! Teachers are creating anchors for their students all the time.

Become aware of the effect you are having on your students. Notice the anchors you use and notice the response of your students. Be sure the learnings you create are the ones you want!

Wednesday—How to Anchor

As you get to know your students, you begin to notice what they look and sound like when they are experiencing frustration, helplessness, success, etc. You can establish an anchor for an experience, such as success, and then use that anchor to bring back the experience of success at a time when they are experiencing frustration or helplessness.

Notice facial expression, voice tone, skin color, breathing rate, etc. When you think the student is most intensely experiencing the feeling, anchor it with a touch, word, gesture, voice tone, wink, etc. Choose an anchor you will be able to reproduce exactly (the touch should be the in the same place with the same pressure). Then at another time, perhaps when the student is going to begin a difficult task, use the anchor. Notice the change as he responds to the anchor by experiencing his feeling of success and beginning the task.

Today, choose one child and anchor a positive experience—success, confidence, joy—even if it is just a wink in a moment of shared laughter. You may realize that you have been anchoring all along without knowing it.

Thursday—Collapsing Anchors

You can create new anchors that collapse or overpower the old ones. If two anchors are simultaneously associated with the same event, the more powerful anchor will prevail, or integration will occur and the new response will be a result of the two previous ones. In the example of the boy who feels terrible when he makes a mistake, you can collapse that anchor by overpowering it with the anchor you have established through the words, voice tone, and facial expression you use to praise him. He feels good when you praise him, he feels terrible when he makes a mistake. So the next time he does make a mistake, smile at him and say, "How wonderful! Now I know what you need to learn. This makes my job easier." The good feeling can be associated with mistakes in the future. He may then be able to use a mistake as a doorway to learning!

Friday—How To Use Anchoring

We have an effect on our students. We can't change that. What we can do is become aware of our power and be responsible in our use of it. Used with love and respect for the individual, anchoring can be a powerful tool for growth.

When teaching, involve the children in auditory, visual, and kinesthetic (feeling) experiences so what they have learned will be anchored in all senses and can be recalled in all senses.

Anchor a learning to the situations where the student will most use it. Further pace or bridge to other situations where the learning could be applied.

Use your words, voice tone and expressions to give encouragement, support and praise. And have fun!

I encourage, support, and praise.

Week of _____

MONDAY	Gather Resources	Anchors I'll use:
	Time: _____	
TUESDAY	One Time Learning	Anchors I've noticed
	Time: _____	
WEDNESDAY	How To Anchor	My experience with anchoring:
	Time: _____	
THURSDAY	Collapsing Anchors	Student response I'd like to change:
	Time: _____	
FRIDAY	Using Anchoring	Plans:
	Time: _____	

WEEK 33

Strategies—Teaching How To Learn

Once you can detect eye accessing scanning patterns and representation systems through listening for predicates, look for recurring sequences of accessing cues (auditory, visual, kinesthetic, etc). For example, a child says, "When I **see** the work (eyes up right), I **say** I just can't do it (eyes down left) and I **feel** afraid (eyes down right)." This pattern (V) visual—(A) auditory—(K) kinesthetic—is a strategy he may use in many area of his life. He may see Reggie Jackson hit a home run, say to himself he wants to do that too, and feel excited, visualize himself doing it, say to himself, "I'm great," and feel proud of himself. This is just one of many possible strategies. Most people have a few strategies they use for many things.

Monday—How To Use Strategies

Why is it that a child is successful one year and not the next? He may have had great teachers both years, but his strategies matched his teacher's one year and didn't match the next year.

The more a child can use all representation systems to perceive and process information, the more he can learn.

The more, and the more varied, his strategies are, the more he can learn.

So, when you teach the group:

1. **Teach to all the children**, tell them, show them, let them feel and experience what they are learning. Teach them many strategies—they will choose what they can use best.

2. When your students are using or practicing concepts learned, have a variety of activities available to them. Let them choose—reports, graphing, outlining, visual aids, experiments, etc. Provide both individual and group work.

Today, choose one of these ideas and plan a change in your teaching strategy.

Tuesday—Outcome Strategy

This is a useful overall teaching strategy.

1. Think of the goal or outcome you want you students to achieve. State it in sensory based terms—what you will be able to see and hear them doing.

2. Decide what skills are necessary for them to be able to learn this.

3. Keeping a positive attitude that your class will be able to achieve, teach those necessary skills, all the while noticing their behavior. Teach in all sensory systems and provide varied experiments for practice.

4. As you notice the response you are getting, match it to your desired outcome. If it matches—you are done! Congratulate them and yourself. If it doesn't match, what resources or skills, attitudes, etc. are needed? Add those and teach again.

5. After trying three or four times, if you still have not achieved your outcome, you may decide to choose a different goal.

Today, choose one lesson you want to teach and use this outcome strategy to achieve your goal.

Wednesday— Chunking

Here is a specific teaching strategy for Part 3 of yesterday's strategy.

1. Chunking

   a. decide what are the parts, the smaller steps, of what you are teaching.

   b. teach these parts (in sequence, if possible).

   c. string all these parts together and "streamline" it until it is a working whole.

   d. give practice until they are able to do it automatically.

2. Teach how to know when to use what they have learned. Anchor this new skill to something that will occur naturally in their environment. For example, if you have just taught them how to choose between "was" and "were," tie this skill to creative writing, proofreading, sentence composition, etc.

3. Teach what to do with the results of what they can now do (after they've learned to add and subtract, teach them to add up purchases and make change). When possible, have them looking for answers to real life problems—such as cutting a recipe in thirds and then making it!

Today, choose one lesson and follow this sequence.

Two plus two is...

I use strategies to reach **all** children.

Thursday—General Design Of Strategies

Each skill can be learned via many different strategies. Some strategies are better than others for learning a particular skill. Visual thinking is useful in imagining abstract concepts. First work with a concrete representation and then a visual image of the concept. Visual thinking is useful in math, word recognition, spelling, reasoning, nonverbal communication, and problem solving.

Auditory thinking is sequential. It is useful in reading comprehension, following directions, verbal communication, and expressive writing.

Kinesthetic thinking is useful in learning motor tasks. We can improve our handwriting as we improve our kinesthetic memory of how to correctly hold the pencil and form letters.

Even though a learning strategy relies more on one sensory area, all sensory areas must be included for a complete strategy. For example, in spelling, a child "hears" the word, "pictures" the spelling, and "feels" whether or not it is correct.

Today, begin noticing which ways of thinking are the most important to the task you teach. Think of possible strategies to teach those tasks.

Depending on the sophistication of the group, you may want to begin discussing with your class—what strategies do they use for a specific task. Pay special attention to the strategies of the students who are successful. These strategies are good ones to teach to students who experience difficulty.

Friday—Working With An Individual's Strategy

If an individual is having difficulty, find out what his most used strategy is, then package information just for him—making use of his strategy. You have detected that whenever you ask Bobby a question, he looks down left (A), up right (V), and down right (K). Teach him by telling him something (A), showing him a visual representation of it (V), and letting him get a feel for it (K) by using the chart to answer questions. Also ask him questions in his sequence. "Bobby, when you **hear** the word "evaporate" and **imagine** the water going back into the air—what would the **feeling** of drying air on your skin be?"

You can also work with a child's strategy to modify it so they will be able to learn from different teachers. Use **his** strategy to teach him different strategies! In the example of Bobby—if he gets a teacher who "leads" with charts, picture, etc. and talks, he won't get information until she talks. So teach him to use self talk about her pictures. Say, "Bobby, when I talk to you with pictures (show the picture) you can get a feel for what I'm saying with the picture by talking to yourself about what you see." Then give him practice by (A) telling him to look at pictures (V), letting him get a feel (K) for what he sees and describe it. Then have him relate what he said to himself with what you teach about the picture or chart so he will, in effect, be "hearing" the picture!

Today, choose a child to "play" with. Determine his strategy through checking eye accessing patterns and spoken predicates. Then design your lesson to reach him. Notice what happens.

Area	Important Ways of Thinking	Possible Strategies
note taking from a lecture	listening—visual organization	A—V—K Make pictures of my words, does it feel right?
math—problem solving	Visualize process, tell self steps, does it feel right?	V—A—K

Week of _____

MONDAY	How To Use Strategies	Lesson _____ I will:
	Time: _____	
TUESDAY	Outcome	Lesson:_____ Outcome:_____ Skills:_____ Response:_____
	Time: _____	
WEDNESDAY	Chunking	Lesson:_____ 1. Chunk, teach, string together, streamline, practice 2. Trigger 3. Teach how to use results
	Time: _____	
THURSDAY	General Design (group discussion)	Something new **I** want to learn: Sensory areas needed in strategy
	Time: _____	
FRIDAY	Working With Individuals	Student: Student's strategy: Plan: Results:
	All day	

WEEK 34

Motivating Strategies—Helping Others Be Successful

You have probably tried many ways to motivate your students. Some worked with some students, and some students you just couldn't reach.

Monday—Motivating Individual Students

In order to reach all students, when teaching the whole group, teach in all systems. Each child will have his own motivator—a feeling, an image, words, etc. So include them all, in order to provide a motivating stimulus for all.

When planning to motivate an individual student, try reversing his own strategy. If Bobby's main strategy is V-A-K, motivate him by describing how it will feel (K) to be listening (A) to a description of a chart (V) showing a new math formula.

Some children have an inverse strategy. They will do what you tell them not to do. This will be an exercise for your creativity—to create a situation where the child "wins" by doing what you want him to do. For example, Jason doesn't want to wear his glasses. He gets a point when he remembers to put them on first, you win a point when you have to remind him.

Today, choose a child to practice these principles on. Have fun!

Tuesday—Relevance As Motivation

Let the children know the importance of what they're learning. Discuss how it will benefit them and/or others. They may even come up with benefits you hadn't thought of!

Tie their new lessons to what they've already learned. Show them the logical relationship between the new and old learning.

Today, choose and discuss relevance, importance, benefits, relationships, etc. Notice any difference in your students' enthusiasm and performance?

Wednesday—Decision As Motivation

Deciding to want something is an excellent motivator. A good decision strategy is:

1. List alternatives.

2. Imagine each alternative in order. Visualize it, notice what you would hear, feel, etc. Just notice at this point, don't decide yet.

3. Imagine each again, and this time, feel "about" each alternative. "How do I feel about this one?"

4. Choose the one that you "feel" is best.

Teach this to your students. Remember to chunk it, tie it to a natural stimulus, and teach them how to use the results. Clearly lay out alternatives for your students and guide them in this strategy. Often students will be highly motivated toward a self chosen goal.

Thursday—Goal Setting As Motivation

Help your students define their goal for a particular lesson. Having a goal in mind during a lesson increases learning. Intending to remember something for a **long** time increases memory. (You are more likely to remember the name of someone you know you will be meeting again.)

So, when presenting spelling words, tell your students to remember the words for the test on Friday **and** the writing they will do in the future. Tell them to learn it well now, and they will have it rest of their lives and won't have to learn it again!

Today, choose a lesson and set goals for it. Refer back to the goals as you teach to keep the goals firmly in their minds.

Friday—Motivating Affirmations And Self Image

Children are naturally motivated to achieve to the level of their belief in themselves. A child who believes he is a B student will do B work. Help your children raise their belief in themselves through affirmations and self-image.

Have your students create and use affirmations about their ability to learn easily, to complete their work, to perform well, etc.

Have them create an "image book" of how they'd like to be. Cut words, and pictures from magazines to describe the image they want to create for themselves. Include skills, material possessions, relationships, achievements, etc.

Today, choose one of these projects and begin.

I motivate myself and others to personal excellence.

Week of _____

MONDAY	Teach to all	Plan: Results:
	Time: _____	
TUESDAY	Relevance	Lesson: Relevance:
	Time: _____	
WEDNESDAY	Decision Strategy	Use the decision strategy for decisions in your own life beginning today.
	Time: _____	
THURSDAY	Goal Setting	Lesson: Goals:
	Time: _____	
FRIDAY	Affirmations and Image Book	Write an affirmation for yourself:
	Time: _____	

WEEK 35

Thinking Strategies—Increase Your Brain Power

Thinking is the object of teaching. Teach a child to think and he can learn the rest of his life. This week we will examine **some** thinking strategies. There are many!

Monday—Eliciting Thinking Strategies

You have some students who are very successful at doing things. Learn their strategy and teach it to others. You can elicit or discover their strategy  by asking them how they do it, and then noticing not what they say, but their eye accessing cues and the predicates they use in their speech. If a child is successfully doing something, the individual steps will probably be out of his conscious awareness and he will be doing it automatically.

A simple strategy (V-A-K) to do an arithmetic problem might be "I look at the problem (V) decide what to do (talk about the process) and do it." Some strategies will be short—some will be longer. Choose the shorter ones to teach other children. They will be less cumbersome. Make sure that all systems (V-A-K) are used—that they check reality after every few steps so they don't get lost in their minds, and be sure they have their outcome defined in the first steps. Don't let them get lost in a loop between two systems (visualize something, feel about it, visualize, feel, V, K, V, K, etc).

To begin, elicit a strategy from one child today. Choose a cooperative student and give yourself uninterrupted time.

When you have the strategy, "talk" him through it and notice his reaction. He will let you know through movement, expression, sound, etc. if it is correct.

Pay attention to the process he is going through, not the content of what he is doing. He will be paying attention to the content.

You may eventually be able to detect a child's strategy by watching him work on a task you've given. Notice how your students look up, move their lips, and wiggle around while they work. This may be a sign of thinking, not playing around!

Tuesday—Change A Thinking Strategy

You can change a child's ineffective strategy in several ways.

1. If a child has a long, cumbersome strategy that does not work, determine what can be done in a more efficient way and change only that part. Teach him the new strategy by rehearsing it or by anchoring in the revised part at the appropriate place.

2. Have two students work together on one process, such as a long division problem. Each child does a part. By working together, they will have the opportunity to pick up each other's strategy.

3. Teach a new strategy to do the same thing. If a child's strategy seems unworkable, teach him a new one you've noticed a more successful student using.

Change a child's strategy in steps. Don't try to make big changes all at once. Change part of it now and more in a few months. Change as little as possible. Thoroughly examine the strategy and make the smallest change possible that will achieve the desired result.

Be sure to test the new strategy and find out if the student is using it automatically.

Wednesday—Teaching Organized Thinking Strategies

To facilitate understanding, teach the overall organizational structure:

1. Teach the organization of the text book—contents, index, preface, introduction, etc. Also teach how chapters are organized. Are topics presented in dark type? Are there summaries? How are important ideas highlighted?

2. Give lectures from notes on the chalkboard or outline handouts. Teach your students to add details while they take notes. Give them clues so that they know what details are important.

3. Teach your students to highlight, outline, and summarize written material.

4. Present an overall structure in a picture, chart, graph, or some other visual aid. Teach each piece and then relate it back to the whole. This is a good technique for math processes.

To begin, choose one lesson today and teach it using one of these principles.

Thursday—Generalization Thinking Strategy

Generalize   Predict   Counter example

Prerequisites for this strategy are:

1. An ability to detect differences in auditory, visual and kinesthetic sensory modes.

2. An ability to notice patterns.

> **Generalize**—the first step in this strategy is to form a generalization about a recurring pattern.

Predict—Based on this generalization, what do you predict will happen? Notice what actually happens. If the results are not as predicted, look for new pattern and form a modified generalization.

Counter example—If the results are as predicted, look for a counter example. Try every way you can break the generalization. If it holds up to this examination, include the generalization in your "belief system" until it proves ineffective or you choose to reexamine it.

If it breaks down, look for new patterns and form a new generalization. Present this strategy in a way that will have meaning for your students. Use examples from their experience or the content area you are teaching.

Friday—Questioning Thinking Strategy

Teach your students to ask more questions. Demonstrate different types of questions and give them practice in using them.

1. Factual recall—what was the man's name?
2. Memory of Detail—what color was the hat?
3. Infer, Presuppose—what was he thinking at the time?
4. Give Examples—Give an example of how he tried to find the treasure.
5. Use what you know to guess what will come next—what do you think will happen?
6. Theorize—what was he trying to prove when he did that?
7. Hypotheses—what could he do to solve his problem?
8. Evaluate and Judge—what was the best thing he did that Christmas?

Teach your students that some questions have "right" answers and some questions have guesses or opinions.

Get your students to wonder!

I teach my students to think.

Week of _____

MONDAY	Eliciting Strategies	Student: Learning task: Strategy:
	Time: _____	
TUESDAY	Change a Strategy	Results:
	Time: _____	
WEDNESDAY	Organizational Structure	Lesson: Organizational structure:
	Time: _____	

THURSDAY	Generalization Strategy	Use this strategy yourself—
		    notice a pattern
		    generalize
		    predict
		    look for counter examples

	Time: _____	
FRIDAY	Active Questioning	Results:
	Time: _____	

The objective of teaching is thinking.

WEEK 36

Learning Strategies—Learning How To Learn

Being aware of something is not the same as learning it. You can be intellectually aware of new habits in some area (like exercise, diet, smoking, getting places on time, etc.) yet you don't change simply by knowing it. You have to want to learn new habits, know **how** to learn them, practice and be **convinced** you can do it, and **use** those habits in their **proper place** in your life.

Monday—Learning Strategy

An overall strategy for learning is:

1. Motivation—want to learn, to change
2. Outcome—know what to learn
3. How—know how to learn it
4. Convincing—know that I've learned it and believe I can do it!
5. Bridging—know when and where to do it
6. Feedback—use it and modify through feedback

This strategy is useful not only for you to use with your students, but also for you to use with yourself, and for your students to use with themselves.

Today, outline the learning strategy on the chalkboard and teach an appropriate lesson, relating it to the learning strategy. Begin teaching your students to learn how to learn.

Tuesday—Learning Attitude

To direct your students to an attitude conducive to learning:

1. Help them to feel successful:

　　a. Use posters, slogans, display excellent work.

　　b. Teach them to pretend, to act as if they already could.

　　c. Keep the goal or outcome in mind and imagine it achieved—feel the feelings of the goal complete and the benefits resulting.

2. Teach your students to focus their attention and screen out distractions.

3. Make their learning relevant by:

　　a. discussing its importance

　　b. relating it to past knowledge.

These attitudes will provide students with motivation and keep their minds on their outcome.

Choose a lesson today and apply these principles. Notice the results.

Wednesday—Learning Strategy Design

Teach your students **how** to do something and then do it. Practice without prior learning does not teach, e.g. **teach** spelling skills using nonsense words, the apply it using real words. Teach the process—then use content.

To design a learning strategy for a specific skill, think:

1. What input or information is needed? What sensory modes are best fitted to take in this information?

2. How can they best process this information? How can they think?

3. What do they have to do with the result? (Keep the outcome in mind.)

4. What feedback is needed to adjust their behavior?

5. What is the best sequence to achieve this?

Make sure that:

1. The outcome is specified at the beginning of the strategy.

2. All sensory systems are involved. (V, A, K)

3. There are checks back to the external environment every few steps.

4. There are no two point loops—(e.g., V-A-V-A-V-A)

5. When a feeling provides a decision, be sure positive feelings are compared, not negative feelings.

Today, choose something you will teach and design a learning strategy for it. Go through the strategy yourself and notice if it would work for you. Plan to teach it tomorrow.

Thursday—Install A Strategy

You can install a strategy in many ways:
1. By rehearsing it, by going through the many steps again and again

2. By demonstrating it and letting your students observe others going through it.

3. By having your students talk each other through it (the one who acts as teacher learns too!).

4. By having your students talk themselves through it.

5. Indirectly by asking them questions in the proper sequence (When I say the word and you visualize how it is spelled, does it feel right to you?).

Choose one or several of these methods and install the strategy you designed yesterday.

Friday—Bridging A Learning Strategy

To build a bridge from what your students learn to where they will use it, anchor their learning to the context in which they will use it. Tell them when and how they can use it. Then have them imagine themselves using it in several example situations.

Give them actual practice using it in several natural situations. Give them tasks where they must use their new skill to accomplish something else or to win a game. Have them practice until they have overlearned it.

Space the practice out over time—some today and some on other days.

Offer feedback so they can learn to modify their behavior.

Teach them to notice the results and provide their own feedback.

Today, anchor the strategy you taught yesterday to natural contexts where it will be useful. Give them practice to begin using it. Plan future practice and write it in your lesson plan book.

I can learn new things!

Week of _____

MONDAY	Learning Strategy	Use the strategy to learn something for yourself motivation: Outcome or goal:
	Time: _____	
TUESDAY	Attitude And Attention	Believe you can do it! Imagine yourself having done it. Write three benefits. 1. 2. 3.
	Time: _____	
WEDNESDAY	Strategy Design	Design a strategy to achieve your goal or Find someone who can do it and find out their strategy.
	Time: _____	
THURSDAY	Install a Strategy	Rehearse your strategy— Teach it to others— Act as if you can— and do it!
	Time: _____	
FRIDAY	Bridging, Practice, and Feedback	Imagine yourself doing it in three situations. 1. 2. 3. Practice—do it! Notice what happens . . .
	Time: _____	

WEEK 37

Convincing Strategies—How We Know That We Know

How do you know when you know something? Do you feel it? Do you see clearly that you've accomplished it? Do you hear it affirmed—"Well done," "I did it"?

Monday—How Do You Know

Ask several students, "How do you know that's right?" "How do you know that?" Notice their eye movements. Some will "see", "hear" or "feel" the correctness or wrongness of it. Give your students practice in last week's strategy lesson or in another lesson. Have them "guess" whether each item is right or wrong. Then check it and notice how close they came. Praise them for knowing when it is wrong. After all, you can't correct something if you don't know it's wrong.

Tuesday—Believing

Often we can do something and not believe we can, or realize that we are doing it, until it is brought to our attention by someone else in chance remarks. And **then** we believe it. Often we believe someone else could accomplish something we are trying to do, but we can't believe **we** could accomplish it.

Create situations where children get a chance to tell each other, "You can do it!" or "You did it!"

1. Have them work in pairs or small groups—perhaps in competition with other groups.

2. Allow only "put ups" or compliments and allow **no** "put downs."

3. Encourage your students to compliment others.

4. Use "brag time" for children to acknowledge their accomplishments honestly.

5. Pair students of like ability to "teach" each other. Teach them to be truly helpful—to encourage someone to do something and praise them when they do it.

6. Give awards for accomplishments of all kinds—not just for the highest grades.

7. Have a system where students can write a compliment or acknowledge growth in someone. (Awareness of others' strengths will help children see their own strengths.)

8. In grading papers, stress how much was learned—not how many were wrong.

9. Continue weekly Success Folders, and have children list accomplishments for the week.

Begin today—choose at least one technique and incorporate it into your teaching.

Wednesday—Feedback Strategy

For anything we do, we need a feedback strategy to know if we've been effective. In communication, we notice the reaction of others. In math, we check for correctness. In science, we do experiments and "prove" something.

When teaching feedback strategies, use one sensory system to verify others. Most people use a kinesthetic response—"it just feels right." An example would be to look at a word you've just written and "feel" if it is spelled correctly.

Today, for at least one lesson, teach a feedback system for your students to use as they practice what they've learned.

Thursday—Testing

Test your students when you've taught them something so you have feedback on the effectiveness of your lessons.

The best test is—do they use it when a situation occurs naturally? Provide situations where your students will have to decide to use the learning—do it—and present the result correctly. Have this as your goal, and make written tests as much like it as possible.

Today, design a test to get feedback on a recent lesson. Use the feedback to modify future lessons.

Friday—Teaching/Learning Strategy

Today, in putting together the teaching and learning strategy, design a lesson.

1. Your teaching or learning outcome:

2. What skills are necessary?

3. Assume success and teach the lesson—

    a.   Motivation:
    b.   Outcome:
    c.   How—learning strategy
    d.   Convincing
    e.   Bridging
    f.   Proofing

4. Notice the response you are getting. Are you achieving your outcome? Modify your lesson and reteach or congratulate yourself on a job well done!

I can help children believe in themselves.

Week of _____

MONDAY	How Do You Know?	How do you know when you know something?
	Time: _____	
TUESDAY	Believing	Believe the most for others—whatever you believe for them, you can believe for yourself!
	Time: _____	
WEDNESDAY	Proofing— Feedback Strategy	Lesson: Results: In the future, I will:
	Time: _____	
THURSDAY	Collapsing Anchors	Student response I'd like to change:
	Time: _____	
FRIDAY	Put It All Together	CONGRATULATIONS!
	Time: _____	

WEEK 38

Where Do We Go From Here?

Monday—Successes!

Review the year—You have had many. List 10 them here:

A+

eacher

1._____

2._____

3._____

4._____

5._____

6._____

7._____

8._____

9._____

10._____

Tuesday—Interests

Today, list those things that you were interested in pursing further—books to read, strategies to design, games to teach specific skills:

Future

1._____

2._____

3._____

4._____

5._____

Wednesday—Problems Into Challenges

Problems:

1._____

2._____

3._____

Challenges:

1._____

2._____

3._____

Thursday—Dreams and Goals

Keeping that feeling of success—review your interests and challenges and dream for your future. List your professional goals here:

1._____

2._____

3._____

4._____

5._____

6._____

7._____

8._____

9._____

10._____

I can
do it!

Friday—Plan Your Strategy

As you think of achieving your goals, plan your strategy:

A. Define your outcome

B. Decide what skills are necessary for achievement

C. Design a strategy to learn those skills or find someone who has the skill and discover how they did it.

Begin today by choosing one of your goals.

My Outcome:

_____

_____

Necessary Skills:

_____

_____

How I will learn them:

_____

_____

Steps to achieve my goal:

1._____

2._____

3._____

Now sit back, relax, and imagine yourself
achieving each one . . .

Week of _____

MONDAY   Success!   Skills I want to acquire:

TUESDAY   Interests of Mine

WEDNESDAY   Problems into
                    Challenges

THURSDAY   Dreams and Goals

FRIDAY   Plan Strategy

I create myself to achieve my goals.

The models taught in this book are not "truths." They are generalizations. They will work. If they don't—do something else! Act as if they are true, but remember they aren't.

Glossary

AFFIRMATIONS
Positive statements to be repeated in order to overcome the mind's natural resistance.

ANCHOR
A specific perception (sight, sound, touch, smell, taste) that consistently brings back the memory of a specific experience.

ANCHORING
Marking an experience with a specific perceptual stimulus in order to recreate the original experience at another time.

BRIDGING
Linking a learned skill to the situations where it will be used.

CHUNKING
Breaking something down into smaller, more easily learned units.

COMPLEX EQUIVALENCES
Connecting two or more unrelated thoughts in the belief they are related. E.g., "It's a sunny day" and "I feel good" becomes "I only feel good on sunny days."

CONTEXTUALIZE
Putting a skill into the context in which it will be used.

DELETE
Leaving something out of conscious awareness.

DISTORTION
To place our own interpretation or perspective on sensory data coming in, thereby causing us to sense something other than what is there.

ELICIT
To discover a person's strategy.

EYE CUES
Eye movements that give clues to a person's thought processes.

GENERALIZATION
To form a belief based on noticing a connection or pattern. Each person has their own way of doing this.

INSTALL
Teach someone a new strategy.

INTENTIONS
The core wish or need behind a person's behavior. This core wish is almost always positive in nature, although the means they choose to satisfy it may not be positive.

LEAD
Changing your behavior to encourage someone to follow your example.

MATCH
Imitating someone's posture, voice tone, breathing, etc. Used to establish rapport and as a prelude to leading.

NOMINALIZE
To turn a verb or a process into a noun.

OUTCOME
Goal.

POLARITY RESPONSE
An automatic response in opposition to whatever is presented.

POSITION OF COMPETENCE
Body position associated with remembered times of being successful and competent.

POSITIVE INTENT
No matter what a person's actions are, he has a positive intent, a desire to do something good for himself.

PRESUPPOSE
To speak or act as if something were already agreed upon as true. E.g., "Are the men from Mars green or blue?" presupposes there are men from Mars.

PROOFING
Using feedback to correct behavior.

REFRAMING
To put something into a different context, or to give it a different interpretation.

RESOURCES
The abilities people naturally possess.

STRATEGIES
Thinking sequences.

STREAMLINE
Combining learning units into a smooth, automatic activity.

SYNESTHESIA
Crossing and blending perceptual modalities.

THINKING
The combinations of present and remembered perceptions.

UTILIZATION
Using to advantage whatever presents itself.

Resources

BOOKS

Anderson, Jill. *Thinking, Changing, Rearranging*. Portland, OR: Metamorphous Press, 1988.

Bandler, Richard and John Grinder. *The Structure of Magic, Vol. I.* Science and Behavior Books, 1975.

Bandler, Richard and John Grinder. *The Structure of Magic, Vol. II.* Science and Behavior Books, 1976.

Bandler, Richard and John Grinder. *Frogs Into Princes*. Moab, Utah: Real People Press, 1979.

Bandler, Richard and John Grinder. *Trance-formations: Neurolinguistic Programming and the Structure of Hypnosis*. Moab, Utah: Real People Press, 1981.

Castillo, Gloria A. *Left Handed Teaching*. Fort Worth: Holt, Rinehart, and Winston, 1978.

Cleveland, Bernard. *Master Teaching Techniques*. Lawrenceville, GA: The Connecting Link Press, 1987.

DeMille, Richard. *Put Your Mother On The Ceiling*. New York: Penguin Books, 1976.

Dilts, Robert. *Applications of NLP*. Cupertino, California: Meta Publications, 1983.

Dilts, Robert, Richard Bandler, John Grinder, Leslie Cameron-Bandler, and Judith DeLozier. *Neurolinguistic Programming I*. Cupertino, California: Meta Publications, 1979.

Gordon, David. *Therapeutic Metaphors: Helping Others Through the Looking Glass*. Cupertino, California: Meta Publications, 1978.

Hendricks, Gay and Thomas B. Roberts. *The 2nd Centering Book*. Englewood, NJ: Prentice Hall, 1989.

Grinder, Michael. *Righting The Educational Conveyor Belt*. Portland, OR: Metamorphous Press, 1989.

Jensen, Eric. *Super Teaching*. Del Mar, CA: Turning Point for Teachers, 1988.

Laborde, Genie. *Ninety Days to Communication Excellence*. Palo Alto, CA: Syntony Publishing, 1985.

Lee, Scout. *The Excellence Principle*. Portland, OR: Metamorphous Press, 1985.

Lewis, Byron and Frank Pucelik. *Magic of NLP Demystified*. Portland, OR: Metamorphous Press, 1982.

Marvell-Mell, Linnaea. *Basic Techniques, Book I*. Portland, OR: Metamorphous Press, 1989.

Oaklander, Violet. *Windows To Our Children*. Moab, Utah: Real People Press, 1989.

O'Connor, Joseph. *Not Pulling Strings*. Portland, OR: Metamorphous Press, 1989.

Wright, Clifford. *Basic Techniques, Book II*. Portland, OR: Metamorphous Press, 1989.

Van Nagel, C., Robert Siudzinski, MaryAnn & Ed Reese. *Mega-Teaching and Learning*. Largo, FL: Southern Institute Press, 1985.

Index

Red Seal
Educational
Series

Classroom Magic
Amazing Technology for Teachers and Home Schoolers
Linda Lloyd

This skillfully crafted workbook of 38 weeks of lesson plans shows teachers and parents advanced communication techniques targeted for behavior, perception and learning. Practical and valuable for classroom and home schooling; adaptable for all ages. ISBN 1-55552-014-6 Pbk.

Not Pulling Strings
Joseph O'Connor

This book explains how NLP and Alexander Technology can improve the teaching, learning, and performing of musical instruments. Learn the integration of language and body awareness for performance excellence. Use both sides of your brain and enjoy music at a new level. ISBN 1-55552-000-6 Pbk.

Righting The Educational Conveyor Belt, 2nd Ed.
Michael Grinder

The comprehensive NLP workbook for teachers at all levels. This book outlines patterns of excellence, techniques for classroom management, and tips on individualized learning styles. ISBN 1-55552-036-7 Pbk.

Thinking, Changing, Rearranging—
Improving Self-Esteem in Young People
Jill Anderson

The ever-popular guidebook to help children wipe out negative self-beliefs ("junk-thought") and build self-esteem. Based on principles of NLP and Rational-Emotive Therapy and filled with exercises and illustrations. Over 275,000 copies in print. ISBN 0-943920-30-2 Pbk.

Positive Change Guides Series

POSITIVE
CHANGE
GUIDES

Get The Results You Want—
A Guide To Communication Excellence For The Helping Professional
Kim Kostere & Linda Malatesta
This book offers the knowledge and NLP skills necessary to make the process of personal change exciting and rewarding. It provides all people who work in innerpersonal communication and changework with sound, step-by-step processes for more effective results. ISBN 1-55552-015-4 PB

Magic of NLP Demystified—
A Pragmatic Guide To Communication And Change
Byron Lewis & Frank Pucelik
This introductory NLP book gives readers a clear and understandable overview of the subject. It covers the basic concepts of NLP using "user-friendly" illustrations and graphics. This is one of the best introductory books available for new NLP students. ISBN 1-55552-017-0 PB

Fitness Without Stress—
A Guide To The Alexander Technique
Robert M. Rickover
This book explains the Alexander Technique, recognized today to be one of the most powerful methods of improving body movement and coordination as well as overall health. It is also a guide to finding and Alexander teacher. No previous experience necessary. ISBN 0-943920-32-9 Cloth

The Power of Balance—
A Guide To A Rolfing View of Health
Brian Fahey, Ph.D.
The importance of balance in life is the emphasis of Fahey's book. It expands on the original ideas about balancing body structure, known as "Rolfing." Reading this thought-provoking text can be a step toward achieving high levels of energy and well-being. ISBN 0-943920-52-3 Cloth

---

Skill Builder Series

The Excellence Principle
Scout Lee, Ed.D.
This standard in the field of NLP was originally a set of personal notes and formal thoughts. In its revised form, this workbook is packed with dynamic metaphors, ideas, exercises and visual aidswhich illustrate the introductory principles of Neurolinguistic Programming. ISBN 1-55552-003-0 PB

Basic Techniques, Book I
Linnaea Marvell-Mell
This is the only NLP workbook available for those who wish to refine their NLP skills, people who have read books on the subject or attended seminars but want more. The book comes with a cassette tape and complements another fine introductory NLP book, Magic of NLP Demystified. ISBN 1-55552-016-2 PB

Basic Techniques, Book II
Clifford Wright
This workbook provides additional tools to refine skills learned in Basic Techniques, Book I. Filled with exercises for individual practice or group work, Basic Techniques II provides ongoing skill-building in NLP technology. ISBN 1-55552-005-7 PB

Advanced Techniques
Phill Boas with Jane Brooks
This manual is designed for use by those who have some knowledge of NLP. It is written from the perspective of the trainer/seminar leader, and much of the information is intended to help the group leader assist participants to get maximum benefit from the 50 exercises. ISBN 0-943920-08-6 PB

The Challenge of Excellence—
Learning The Ropes of Change
Scout Lee, Ed.D. & Jan Summers, Ed.D.
Lee and Summers' book is about utilizing challenge and playfulness to program the human computer for excellence. It has sophisticated information on body language and its connection to the mental process. ISBN 1-55552-004-9 PB

Educational Products Available From
Metamorphous Advanced Product Services

BOOKS

More than 30 titles for students, parents, teachers, children, and homeschoolers!
These titles offer valuable information on accelerated learning, classroom management, individual learning styles, mind-mapping, creativity, study techniques, super-learning, super-memory, super-teaching, and self esteem.

CASSETTES

ONE TO GROW ON SERIES
by Trenna Daniells
These exciting, non-violent stories teach self-reliance for children ages 4-12. Dramatized with original music and sound effects, the stories encourage children to approach life with positive attitudes, helping to build self-esteem from an early age. Tapes sold separately or in money-saving book-style sets.

LEARNING FORUM AUDIO COURSES
Success through "alpha writing"

VIDEOS

- Increase math confidence and success
- Build test-taking skills for better grades
- How to take "quantum leaps" in reading speed
- Develop a winning attitude
- Increase memory
- Develop better personal skills for the classroom and relationships with other teachers, students, and parents

LEARNING GAMES

People often learn important teachings when they are having *fun*—and while these learning games teach important lessons, they are enjoyable for children and adults alike, family members and friends.

FutureStories Game—A fun game where you talk about your hopes and dreams for the future. Use your imagination as you discover new ideas! Think about the future; dream to your heart's content.

LifeStories Game—A fun game where you talk about your experiences from the past. Recall funny moments, important times and cherished thoughts. Pass on family history. Laugh and talk with LifeStories, the game that's as full of surprises as life itself.

ZEBU Hypnotic Language Card Game—Zebu is a normal deck of playing cards with 52 extraordinary language patterns taken from the field of NLP and the work of Milton Erickson. Each card in the deck has a language pattern written at the top and bottom, and a commentary in the center. Playing Zebu is learning at its best, because the whole time is spent listening to and using the language patterns—and it's entertaining. Instructions, insightful commentary and examples are included.

Creative Whack Pack—The Creative Whack Pack is a clever idea-generating tool featuring 64 beautiful 5-color cards. Some cards show places to find new information. Some provide techniques to generate new ideas. Some lend decision-making advice. And some give you the kick you need to get your ideas into action. The companion book, *A Whack On The Side of The Head*, opens your mind for innovative thinking. It is filled with provocative puzzles, anecdotes, humor, paradox, exercises, metaphors, scientific facts and general wisdom. This is a fantastic catalyst for "brain-storming" and setting your imagination free!

Metamorphous Press

P.O. Box 10616 Portland, OR 97210
(503) 228-4972 FAX (503) 223-9117

Metamorphous Press is a publisher of books and other media providing resources for personal growth and positive change. MP publishes leading-edge ideas that help people strengthen their unique talents and discover that we are responsible for our own outcomes.

Many of our titles center around Neurolinguistic Programming (NLP). NLP is an exciting, practical, and powerful communication model that has been able to connect observable patterns of behavior and communication and the processes that underlie them.

Metamorphous Press provides selections in many useful subject areas such as communication, health and fitness, education, business and sales, therapy, selections for young persons, and other subjects of general and specific interest. Our products are available in fine bookstores around the world.

Our distributors for North America are:

Baker & Taylor	M.A.P.S.	Pacific Pipeline
Bookpeople	Moving Books	Sage Book Distributors
Ingram	New Leaf	the distributors
Inland Book Co.		

For those of you overseas, we are distributed by:

Airlift (UK, Western Europe)
Specialist Publications (Australia)

New selections are added regularly and availability and prices change, so call for a current catalog or to be put on our mailing list. If you have difficulty finding our products in your favorite bookstore, or if you prefer to order by mail, we will be happy to make our books and other products available to you directly. Please call or write us at:

Metamorphous Press
P.O. Box 10616   Portland, OR 97210-0616
TEL (503) 228-4972
FAX (503) 223-9117

To Order Products or Request A Catalog
Call TOLL FREE
1-800-937-7771

Metamorphous Advanced Product Services

Metamorphous Advanced Product Services (M.A.P.S.) is the master distributor for Metamorphous Press and other fine publishers.

M.A.P.S. offers books, cassettes, videos, software, and miscellaneous products in the following subjects; Bodywork & Fitness (including Alexander Technique and Rolfing), Business & Sales; Children; Education; Enneagram; General Interest; Health & Wellness; Hypnosis; Music/Arts; Personal Development; Psychology (including Neurolinguistics); Relationships/Sexuality; and the work of Virginia Satir.

If you cannot find our books at your favorite bookstore, you can order directly from **M.A.P.S.**

TO ORDER PRODUCTS OR REQUEST A FREE CATALOG:

MAIL   M.A.P.S.
P.O. Box 10616
Portland, OR 97210-0616

FAX   (503) 223-9117

CALL   Toll free 1-800-233-MAPS
(6277)

ALL OTHER BUSINESS:

CALL   (503) 228-4972